Natural Computing Serie

Springer
Berlin
Heidelberg
New York
Hong Kong
London
Milan
Paris
Tokyo

Ronald W. Morrison

Designing Evolutionary Algorithms for Dynamic Environments

With 78 Figures

Springer

Author

Ronald W. Morrison

Mitretek Systems
3150 Fairview Park Drive South
Falls Church, Virginia 22042, USA
ronald.morrison@mitretek.org

Series Editors

G. Rozenberg (Managing Editor)
rozenber@liacs.nl
Th. Bäck, J. N. Kok, H. P. Spaink

Leiden Center for Natural Computing, Leiden University
Niels Bohrweg 1, 2333 CA Leiden, The Netherlands

A. E. Eiben
Vrije Universiteit Amsterdam, The Netherlands

ACM Computing Classification (1998): I.2.8, F.3

ISSN 1619-7127
ISBN 978-3-642-05952-0

Springer-Verlag is a part of Springer Science+Business Media
springeronline.com

© Springer-Verlag Berlin Heidelberg 2010
Printed in Germany

Cover design: KünkelLopka, Heidelberg

Printed on acid-free paper   45/3142GF – 5 4 3 2 1 0

To Peggy, Kimberly, and Erica

Preface

The robust capability of evolutionary algorithms (EAs) to find solutions to difficult problems has permitted them to become popular as optimization and search techniques for many industries. Despite the success of EAs, the resultant solutions are often fragile and prone to failure when the problem changes, usually requiring human intervention to keep the EA on track.

Since many optimization problems in engineering, finance, and information technology require systems that can adapt to changes over time, it is desirable that EAs be able to respond to changes in the environment on their own. This book provides an analysis of what an EA needs to do to automatically and continuously solve dynamic problems, focusing on *detecting* changes in the problem environment and *responding* to those changes.

In this book we identify and quantify a key attribute needed to improve the detection and response performance of EAs in dynamic environments. We then create an enhanced EA, designed explicitly to exploit this new understanding. This enhanced EA is shown to have superior performance on some types of problems. Our experiments evaluating this enhanced EA indicate some previously unknown relationships between performance and diversity that may lead to general methods for improving EAs in dynamic environments. Along the way, several other important design issues are addressed involving computational efficiency, performance measurement, and the testing of EAs in dynamic environments.

This book is based on research submitted in partial fulfillment of the requirements of the degree of Doctor of Philosophy at George Mason University. I would like to thank my dissertation director, Prof. Kenneth A. De Jong, for his support and encouragement, Prof. John Grefenstette, Bill Liles and Dr. Chris Reedy for many stimulating discussions, Dr. Gary Denman for sponsoring some of the early research while he was President of GRCI, and the staff at Springer-Verlag for their kind assistance. Finally, I would like to thank my family and friends for their patience and tolerance during this long process.

Annandale, Virginia, USA   *Ronald W. Morrison*
April, 2004

Contents

1

Introduction

1.1 Overview and Background

1.1.1 Overview

Evolutionary algorithms (EAs) are heuristic, stochastic search algorithms often used for optimization of complex, multi-dimensional, multi-modal functions, where the actual functional form is not known. EAs are adaptive algorithms in the sense that they accumulate and use information to progressively improve their ability to solve some problem of interest. EAs operate by creating a population of potential solutions to a particular problem and evaluating those solutions directly. The mechanism by which an EA accumulates information regarding the problem of interest is an exact evaluation of the quality of each of the potential solutions, using a problem-specific evaluation method, referred to as the fitness function. Various iterative operations, called genetic operators, then improve the quality of the solution by: (1) successive refinement of the best solutions found, and (2) searching the unexplored solution space to identify promising areas containing solutions better than those found so far. Identification of the appropriate balance of exploitation of the best solutions and further exploration of the solution space have been the focus of much research in the EA community.

The robust capability of EAs to find solutions to difficult problems has permitted them to become the optimization and search techniques of choice by many industries. From the design of jet engines [30] to the scheduling of airline crews [39], EAs, in their various forms, are routinely solving a multitude of complex, multi-dimensional, multi-modal optimization problems.

But what happens if the information that has been provided to the EA changes? Despite the obviously successful application of evolutionary techniques to complex problems in many different environments, the resultant solutions are often fragile, and prone to failure when subjected to even minor changes in the problem. In the context of evolutionary computation, a problem with an objective function that changes over time is referred to as having a "dynamic fitness landscape." Since information is accumulated by the EA during successive iterations, there is an implicit assumption of consistency in the evaluation function. Unfortunately, the consistency assumption is not the case in many real problems. A variety of engineering, economic, and information technology problems require systems that adapt to changes over time. Examples of problems where environmental changes could cause the fitness landscape to be dynamic include: target recognition, where the sensor performance varies based on environmental conditions; scheduling problems, where available resources vary over time; financial trading models, where market conditions can change abruptly; investment portfolio evaluation, where the assessment of investment risk varies over time; and data mining, where the contents of the database are continuously updated. These types of problems may experience simple dynamics, where the fitness peaks that represent the optimal problem solution drift slowly from one value to the next, or complicated dynamics, where the fitness peaks change more dramatically, with current peaks being destroyed and new, remote peaks arising from valleys.

The motivation for designing EAs for solving dynamic problems is simple. With the continuing increases in available processing power, it is becoming computationally possible to assign an EA to continuously solve actual dynamic problems without the need for human intervention. This, however, requires that the EA can continuously provide a "satisfactory" level of performance when subjected to a dynamic fitness landscape and, at our current level of understanding, we are not able to ensure such performance. In this book we will discuss research that exploits insights provided by biology and control systems engineering to address issues involved in the design of EAs for dynamic fitness landscapes. The results of this research provide a basis for the improved ability to create EAs that successfully operate in dynamic environments without human intervention.

1.1.2 EAs Described

There are four major classes of EAs: genetic algorithms (GAs), evolutionary strategies (ESs), evolutionary programming (EP), and genetic programming (GP) [5], [33]. Solving a problem with EAs involves ten steps. The differences between the classes of EAs result from a difference in emphasis on, or approach to, some of the ten steps [41], [7], [34].

The ten steps are:

1. Decide on an encoding scheme for the possible solutions to the problem that will permit alternative solutions to be "evolved." This selection of problem representation involves mapping the problem solution space (called phenotypic space) into an equivalent representation (called the genotypic space) that is amenable to application of the operators of an EA. For genetic algorithms, the encoding scheme most often used is bit-strings, whereas evolutionary strategies and evolutionary programming

most often use strings of real numbers for their representation. In genetic programming computer programs are represented as variable-sized trees consisting of arithmetic functions, conditional operators, variables, and constants.

2. Select an initial population size and randomly create an initial population of potential solutions to the problem. The initial population size selection involves tradeoffs between the need to adequately sample the solution space and the need to bound the computational requirements of the EA. In most EAs, the population size, once selected, remains constant during operation. Less traditional implementations involve population sizes that vary.

3. Select an evolutionary architecture. Two main architectures are used in EAs: generational and steady-state. In the generational architecture, there are distinct generations, where all population members are replaced by the succeeding generation. In a steady-state EA, population members are added at the same rate that population members are removed. The most common EA architecture is generational.

4. Evaluate the quality of the solutions in the population. This step involves converting the genotype representation for each member of the population into the phenotype representation for evaluation using an unequivocal evaluation of how "good" the solution is. This is measured by use of a fitness function. The design of an appropriate fitness function for each problem being solved by an EA can be very difficult. When it is not possible to determine an unequivocal gradation of "better" and "worse" for alternative solutions, an EA is not a good choice of method for problem solution.

5. Select the parents of the next generation. This is where the "best" members of the population are selected for the generation of offspring. In EAs, this is the step where the genetic material that will survive to the next generation is determined. In some EA implementations the entire population has offspring. Genetic algorithms usually use a probabilistic rule, based on fitness evaluations, to select parents for the offspring.

6. Mix the genes of the parents to form offspring. This step, called crossover or recombination, is a major focus in the construction of new potential problem solutions in genetic algorithms and genetic programming; it is used to a lesser extent or not at all in evolutionary strategies; and is not used at all in evolutionary programming. Genetic algorithms use a variety of crossover techniques, including 1 to N-point crossover (where N is the length of the genome). In GAs, individual genes are generally left unaltered in their recombination to a new genome. When crossover is used with real-numbered encoding schemes in evolutionary strategies, genes are sometimes recombined to an intermediate value between the values at the crossover points. Crossover techniques usually involve two parents, but schemes have been devised that involve three or more parents.

7. Apply a mutation operator to either modify the offspring just created or create new offspring from the parents. In evolutionary programming and in evolutionary strategies without recombination, this is the method for creating new offspring from the parents. Mutation operators randomly change individual genes of the members of the population. In GAs, mutation is usually fixed at some small uniform probability, whereas for both evolutionary strategies and evolutionary programming, mutation is governed by statistical operators that vary during the operation, based on genetic diversity, fitness, or both.

8. Select which of the offspring survive. This is the primary method of selection for the survival of genetic material in the case of evolutionary strategies and evolutionary programming, where the entire population generates offspring. Evolutionary strategies most commonly use one of two selection methods: a new generation is created from the μ best $(1 \leq \mu \leq \lambda)$ individuals from the set of λ offspring, referred to as (μ, λ) selection; or a new generation is created from the μ best individuals from the union set of λ offspring and their immediate antecedents, referred to as $(\mu + \lambda)$ selection. Evolutionary programming normally involves a tournament selection technique for survival from the union of parents and offspring.

9. Loop through steps 4 through 8 until termination. It is necessary to have some criterion for stopping. Most often, this criterion is a measure of failure to improve over some number of iterations.

10. Repeat steps 1 through 9 a statistically significant number of times. Since the actual results of the EA vary based on the randomly selected initial population and the stochastic genetic operators, EAs are usually run repeatedly with different initial populations until their experimental performance on a problem of interest is statistically established. In actual practice, there are times where one operation will derive a satisfactory solution to a problem at hand, and there is no reason to execute the first nine steps more than once.

The application of these ten steps, in their various forms, has been a research focus for over 25 years [20], [29], [18] and, with the increased performance of commonly available computers, has been the source of solutions to practical engineering and mathematical problems for over ten years. To understand the difficulties anticipated in the analysis of the performance of EAs in dynamic fitness landscapes, we must first briefly review what is known, or at least fairly widely accepted, about the mechanisms by which EAs operate in static fitness landscapes.

When a population is initialized, it randomly samples the solution space for promising areas to pursue. A histogram of the fitness values for this population would illustrate the fitness distribution for the population. If an appropriate encoding scheme has been selected, the problem is well formed, and the population is large enough to adequately sample the solution space, this fitness distribution should have a range of fitness values that is large enough to permit the EA to distinguish between promising areas of the solution space and areas that are less promising. Occasionally, when designing an EA solution for a real problem, it is found that the initial population has fitness values that are all zeros (or all some other value). This situation provides no information to the EA about where to focus the search in the solution space, so an EA in this situation becomes just an inefficient method for random search. Other difficult problems exist where the regions of the search space with increasing fitness lead the EA away from the desired solution. These problems are referred to as deceptive [24].

The parent-selection step determines which genetic material will survive to future generations. Different selection strategies place different emphasis on retention of the genetic material in the best solutions found so far. When using an elitist strategy, for example, the best solutions found are retained in the population at the expense of losing the genetic material present in the lower-fitness population members [40]. Other selection strategies may not exclusively retain the highest fitness members, but merely bias their selection towards the members of higher fitness. It should be noted that important genetic material can be lost during selection, because it was only present in members with relatively low overall fitness.

The two operators which are responsible for the creation of offspring are crossover and mutation. Because its effects are easier to describe, mutation will be discussed first, although, in practice, it is often applied second.

Mutation makes small random changes to the genetic material that has made it through the selection stage. Since mutation rates are generally small and mutation is applied to the genetic material of population members that have already been determined to be relatively highly fit, minor random changes can be visualized as small local searches of a promising area of the solution space. This search, however, is "local" in genotypic space, whereas fitness is measured in phenotypic space. It is easy to envision encoding schemes where minor genetic material changes cause jumps to vastly different areas of the phenotypic solution space. It is also important to notice that many of the studies of the performance of EAs ignore the additional dynamics caused by the genotypic to phenotypic mappings, and focus on problems where this mapping is trivial (such as the ONEMAX problem described in the next paragraph). The point to remember here is that mutation is a local search operator as viewed in genotypic space.

Crossover is the mixing of the genes of the selected parents and is a much more complicated operator. An excellent analysis of the effects of crossover can be found in [62] but we will adopt a simplified explanation here to facilitate conceptual understanding. There are many techniques for mixing the genetic material of the selected parents to form offspring, but the reason that we mix the genetic material is to examine the ability of the genetic material from one highly fit individual to improve the overall fitness of another highly fit individual. This can be illustrated with a trivial, binary-encoded GA attempting to find a string of all ones (known as the ONEMAX problem), where the fitness evaluation is a simple count of the number of ones in the string:

Parent 1: 11110OOO Fitness = 4   Parent 2: OOOO1111 Fitness = 4.

With simple one-point crossover, it is possible for the GA to supplement the genetic material of Parent 1 with that of Parent 2 and create an offspring:

11111111 Fitness = 8.

Of course, in this case it is also possible to create an offspring of fitness zero. It is also possible in other cases for the crossover operator to disrupt good sequences of alleles that existed in one of the parents and are necessary for the solution. In the case of multi-modal fitness landscapes, when mixing the genes of relatively highly fit individuals from the same peak, crossover is essentially a local search operator that is strongly examining the solution space near that peak. If the highly fit parents are from different peaks in a multi-modal landscape, crossover becomes a global search operator. Unfortunately, it is usually not possible to easily identify whether population members are on the same peak in a multi-modal problem due to lack of detailed knowledge of the functional form of the fitness landscape.

Although our theoretical understanding of EA behavior in static fitness landscapes is far from complete (see, for example, [63], [6]), the situation gets much worse when dynamic fitness landscapes are introduced. Dynamic fitness landscapes present the additional problems of detecting and responding to changes in information that the EA has used.

1.2 Previous Research

Early research into EA performance in dynamic fitness landscapes was conducted over ten years ago [25], [14], [27]. Recent years have seen a significant increase in interest in this subject [42], [35], [4], [69], [64], [67], [38], [72], [55], [12]. Despite this increased interest in the performance of EAs in changing environments, the "successes and failures" of EAs in dynamic fitness landscapes that have been reported to date have mostly just measured the speed of the adaptation of some specific EA implementation. This measurement is usually made using a simple example problem and often reported without analysis of the dynamics of the sample problem selected or the generality of any results. As has been shown in the study of EAs in static environments, comparative studies of the effectiveness of various EAs in dynamic environments will require rigorous and standardized test functions. Furthermore, since it is likely that techniques that are successful in improving the performance of EAs in adapting to some types of fitness landscape changes are likely to be less effective in other types of landscape changes, standardized test functions will be required to cover a variety of different types of dynamic behavior.

Until recently, most of the studies of dynamic fitness landscape performance have involved randomly or gradually changing the location of the fitness peak during the progress of a GA and examining the resulting performance of the algorithm. This type of study only answers the question, "How fast can a particular EA solve a particular problem, starting with the population that remains after solving (or partially solving) a different problem with a similar structure?" The answer, not surprisingly, is often "not very well," since finding the new peak location in a fitness landscape involves solution-space exploration, and a partially converged population has already lost some of its genetic diversity and may no longer adequately cover the solution space. When the portion of the search space that is changing is not covered by the population, an EA will not detect that a change in the fitness landscape has occurred, and therefore not alter its behavior to accommodate the change.

Interesting results upon which to initiate this research have been reported in several studies of EAs in dynamic fitness landscapes and in the literature regarding the on-line adaptation of various genetic operators. The previous research potentially applicable to the study of EAs in dynamic fitness landscapes is categorized below in terms of the EA processes.

1.2.1 Diversity Introduction and Maintenance

If a dynamic fitness landscape changes, modifications to EAs that encourage re-exploration, such as increased mutation, should improve performance. These would help re-explore the fitness landscape in the event of a change, so that the new solution, wherever it resides in the fitness landscape, can be discovered.

Some of the more extensive studies of EAs in dynamic fitness landscapes have focused on the introduction of mutation mechanisms for increased solution-space exploration when changes in the solution space are detected. Cobb devised an adaptive mutation operator, called triggered hypermutation, for increasing the genetic search when changes in the fitness landscape are detected [14]. The triggered hypermutation algorithm, as originally published, is based on a standard generational EA, with a fixed population size, proportional selection, N-point crossover, and a small mutation rate (0.001) that is applied uniformly to the population. Where the algorithm differs from standard EAs is that the small mutation rate (called the "base" mutation rate) is not always the mutation rate that is applied to the population. The algorithm is adaptive in that the mutation rate does not remain constant over time. When a change in the fitness landscape is detected, the mutation rate is multiplied by a hypermutation factor before it is applied. If the hypermutation factor is very large ($\sim$1000), the effect of hypermutation is equivalent to re-initializing the population and starting the EA over. Smaller hypermutation factors introduce less diversity into the population.

Grefenstette continued this research [27] and proposed two diversity introduction processes intended to maintain a continuous exploration of the search space while disrupting ongoing search as little as possible: (1) a partial hypermutation step, and (2) the introduction of random immigrants into the population. Both Cobb and Grefenstette examined the performance of an adaptive mutation operator in the context of several different kinds of fitness landscape changes [15].

Another strategy for increasing search after detecting a change in the environment was suggested by Varak [65]. They developed a variable, local-search operator to enable GA-based control systems to track slowly varying solutions to a specific control system problem. As suggested by Cobb, the new search operator is triggered only when the time-averaged best performance of the population deteriorates.

Other EAs depend on adaptive mutation operators, even in static fitness landscapes. Some of these techniques were pioneered by Schwefel and, in their most general form, use a mutation mechanism that enables the algorithm to evolve its own mutation strategy parameters during the search, creating an explicit link between the amount and type of mutation and the fitness of the population [5], [28]. Bäck has also performed an initial evaluation of the performance of evolutionary strategies in dynamic landscapes and illustrated that the performance of evolutionary strategy self-adaptation methods is sensitive to the type of dynamic problem [4].

Finally, an interesting recent study examined the use of variable-length EAs in dynamic environments [73]. The results showed promise on the problems examined, but whether the improved EA performance is due to additional genetic material availability substituting for enhanced diversity or some other effect of the variable-length EA dynamics is uncertain at this time.

1.2.2 Addition of Memory

An early study that combines EAs and case-based reasoning in dynamic environments was conducted by Ramsey and Grefenstette. They applied case-based reasoning to create a history of good solutions for previously encountered cases and, when a change was detected in the environment, the EA was re-started, using these previous cases to seed the initialized population [54].

More recently, several researchers have examined whether the addition of a memory component to an EA is useful in dynamic fitness landscapes of a recurrent nature. A novel modification to the standard (μ, λ) evolutionary strategy was evaluated in [50]. This modification adds adaptive predictors that are based on the parents' memories to the normal adaptive parameters of the ES. Alternative memory addition was suggested by Mori, who combined a thermodynamical genetic algorithm (TDGA), which maintains population diversity by an entropy measure, with a memory-based feature, inspired by natural immune systems, to address changing fitness landscapes with a recurrently varying nature [42]. Diploid representation and polygenic inheritance have been examined as methods for retaining genetic information about previously found, high-quality solutions in dynamic environments by Connor Ryan

[57], [58]. Additional memory mechanisms for use in fitness landscapes where the global optimum frequently revisits the same regions were also examined in [12].

1.2.3 Importance of the Characteristics of the Landscape

While the characteristics of the landscape dynamics would be expected to affect the performance of an EA, few studies have examined this subject in any detail. Wilke examined some of the effects of landscape ruggedness in dynamic environments [69], and Karsten and Nichole Weicker have done some research into varying how much information is available to an EA in a dynamic environment and how the EA exploits that information [67].

With each type of landscape characteristic, there may be a variety of dynamic properties. For example, the magnitude of the change can be large or small, and the speed of the changes can be rapid or slow relative to EA time. Each of these dynamic properties can, in turn, be uniform, periodic, recurrent but aperiodic, random, or chaotic.

The speed of the fitness landscape changes (rapid or slow) relative to EA "time" (measured in generations) is one of the dynamic properties that has only recently received initial systematic study. This dynamic property is referred to as the "landscape change period" (or just "period"), and is defined as the number of EA generations between fitness landscape changes. We have previously performed an initial study of the effects of changing this dynamic characteristic on the performance of Cobb and Grefenstette's triggered hypermutation technique [46].

It should also be noted that for most experiments with dynamic fitness landscapes, dynamics are overlaid onto an underlying static landscape. These static landscapes usually have their own set of attributes that can facilitate or inhibit the EA performance, and the effects of these static attributes are also often poorly understood.

1.3 Open Research Issues

As can be seen in the research described above, the techniques that have been added to EAs to improve their performance in dynamic fitness landscapes have considered only limited types of EA modifications that may be required to achieve success in dynamic landscapes. There has been little analysis of the different types of dynamic fitness landscape problems that may be solved by EAs and also little comparative analysis of the types of EA extensions that may be effective in solving the different types of problems.

There are many open research issues regarding the design of EAs for dynamic fitness landscapes. Among the most fundamental and interesting of these issues are:

1. Improved theoretical understanding of the performance of EAs in dynamic fitness landscapes. The theoretical understanding of EAs in static fitness landscapes is far from mature, but very little is understood about the behavior of EAs in dynamic fitness landscapes.

2. Diversity quantification. While a number of researchers have intuitively focused on increases in diversity to improve EA performance in dynamic fitness landscapes, there has been little research into quantitative identification of the necessary amount of diversity for different types of problems.

3. Diversity measurement for dynamic problems. Although diversity has been identified as an important aspect of EA performance in dynamic landscapes, the concept of diversity for dynamic landscapes has been carried over from studies of static EAs. However, common usage of diversity measures suggests some misunderstanding regarding what aspects of diversity are important to EA performance in dynamic fitness landscapes.

4. Performance measurement. The measurement of the relevant aspects of EA performance in dynamic landscapes is a complex issue and is largely unaddressed in the literature. Results are most often reported in simple graphs over time without any method to determine the overall EA performance, nor the statistical significance of differing results.

5. Exploration of new methods to improve the performance of EAs in practical dynamic fitness landscapes. Biological systems suggest many potential enhancements to EAs that may improve performance in dynamic fitness landscapes that have not been evaluated.

6. Comparative studies. There has not been any comprehensive comparative study of the performance of EA techniques in a controlled, representative suite of dynamic fitness landscapes. For over 20 years, the De Jong test suite [18] has been used to measure the performance of various GAs in function optimization. Additional test functions have been added over time; some of the more frequently encountered ones are known as the Rastrigin, Schwefel, and Griewangk functions. Recently, test generators suitable for use in dynamic environments have started to become available [45], [10]. These test generators are starting to be used to evaluate EA extensions in a variety of dynamic environments.

1.4 Importance and Relevance

Dynamic fitness landscapes are common in a wide variety of problems where EAs are currently being applied. For example, in financial applications, EAs are being used for portfolio balancing, risk analysis, and the identification of trading strategy parameters. Difficulties arise because the underlying behavior of the financial markets and the risk analysis basis change over time. In another example, EAs are being used for data mining in large databases [22]. As these databases change, however, new relationships in the data go unnoticed until the EA-based data-mining effort is performed again. Without effective methods for dealing with dynamic fitness landscapes in these applications and many others, an often-applied current practice is to "periodically" re-run the EA to see if anything has changed. If circumstances have not changed, the effort to re-run the EA was wasted. If circumstances change before the anticipated need to re-run the EA, whatever information the EA was providing is likely to be wrong, and could be very wrong. Awaiting notice that the underlying problem environment has changed through the observation that the system you are using for making business decisions no longer works is often expensive, usually time consuming, and can be disastrous. The ability to allow an EA to continuously provide appropriate solutions to these (and other) changing problems without the need for discontinuous operation or human intervention would improve efficiency in these complex domains.

The research described herein will contribute to the understanding of the performance of EAs in dynamic fitness landscapes. It will examine the applicability and effectiveness of promising EA improvements that were inspired by biological and engineering systems performing in a variety of complex dynamic environments. Along the way, we will address a number of important design issues that will facilitate further research in this area. Several of these issues are related to the methods for determining population diversity and the methods for reporting EA performance. We will also provide a problem generator for dynamic fitness landscape problems that easily delivers a wide range of reproducible dynamic behaviors for EA researchers.

The combination of the resolution of some fundamental design issues with comparative experiments in a variety of dynamic fitness landscapes will provide a step towards the goal of designing EAs to continuously solve important, but changing, problems without human intervention.

1.5 Book Structure

The remainder of this book is structured as follows:

- Chapter 2 will discuss dynamic problems and the characteristics of EAs that are required for effective performance in dynamic environments.
- Chapter 3 will provide some insights from biology and control system engineering regarding methods for exploiting diversity-creating mechanisms to deal with the complexities of dynamic fitness landscapes.
- Chapter 4 will discuss measurement of population diversity and introduce new and efficient methods for computing the traditional measures of population diversity. This chapter will then go on to address significant shortcomings in the use of traditional population diversity measures and provide a new and efficient population diversity measure that corrects these shortcomings.
- Chapter 5 will present the architecture of an extended EA which has been designed to exploit our new understanding of population diversity measurement to improve the performance of the EA in dynamic environments.

Additionally, techniques developed for the creation of this new EA architecture will be addressed in the context of their potential applicability to population initialization techniques for static EAs.

- Chapter 6 will describe the experimental framework for testing this new EA. A new test problem generator will be presented to provide a standardized capability for testing EAs in dynamic landscapes and comparing results. Additionally, this chapter will address shortcomings in common performance measures for comparing results in examining EAs in dynamic fitness landscapes, and provide a performance measure that addresses the shortcomings.
- Chapter 7 will address the issue of performance measurement of EAs in dynamic fitness landscapes and derive appropriate performance reporting measures that cover an EA's exposure to a range of fitness landscape dynamics with results that can be checked for statistical significance.
- Chapter 8 will provide an analysis of the results of the performance of the extended EA, described in Chap. 5, in the dynamic fitness landscape problems described in Chap. 6. This chapter will also identify and analyze discovered relationships between important EA parameters and the resulting EA performance.
- Chapter 9 will return to the techniques developed in Chap. 5 to demonstrate their usefulness in the problem of static EA population initialization.
- Chapter 10 will provide a summary of this research and provide suggestions for future research.

2

Problem Analysis

2.1 Overview

This chapter will examine the subject of non-stationary problems in general, and help focus the remainder of the book on the problems of interest. Specifically, this chapter will examine the types of non-stationary landscapes and the attributes needed by an EA to be successful in these dynamic environments.

2.2 Non-stationary Problems

Non-stationary, or dynamic, problems change over time. The concept of dynamic environments in the context of this book means that the underlying fitness landscape changes during the operation of the EA.

There are a wide variety of possible types of environmental dynamics. Also, sometimes implicit in the definition of dynamic environments, there is uncertainty about the nature of the changes to be expected, the magnitude of the changes, and the duration of any static environmental periods between changes. To the extent that any of these uncertainties can be reduced, customized techniques for dealing with the known change characteristics can be developed. In the presence of uncertainty about these dynamic characteristics, however, it is necessary for any search algorithm operating in the dynamic environment to be flexible enough to enable detection and response to whatever the environment provides.

Since we will be addressing a broad class of dynamic landscape types, it is appropriate here to address potential concerns regarding the "No Free Lunch" theorem of Wolpert and Macready [71]. We are not, in this research, attempting to create a "universal problem solver" for all potentially existent types of dynamic problems. Instead, we will be focusing on the few classes of dynamic problems with dynamic behavior that is likely to be of interest to the users of EAs, and on automated techniques to improve the efficiency of an EA for the problem type it has encountered.

2.3 EA Performance in Dynamic Environments

A number of studies of EAs in dynamic landscapes have been performed, for example [12], [72], [38]. Common to all of these studies is an overview of the performance of a basic EA in a dynamic environment. While different performance measures are used, the same basic characteristics of performance can be seen in all of these studies. Figure 2.1 provides an overview of the basic EA performance in a dynamic environment, with the best fitness found at each generation as the performance measure.

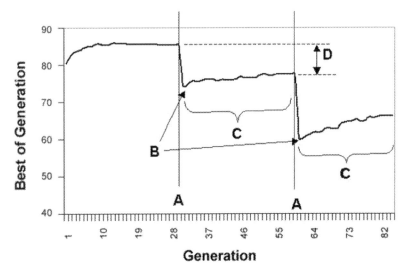

Fig. 2.1. Canonical EA performance in a dynamic environment

As Fig. 2.1 shows, the EA starts performing normally, with the best fitness following a generally upward track, and the EA locating better fitness value by finding and climbing the landscape peaks. This continues until the landscape moves, at point A, and the best-of-generation fitness suddenly drops, as shown at point B in Fig. 2.1. At this point the EA will start to identify the new optimum location and climb the peak. The best-of-generation value starts to climb again, as shown in labeled area C. As long as the EA has enough diversity to start to find the new optimum, this pattern will continue with each landscape change. Without a diversity maintenance technique, the EA tends to "lose ground" with each successive landscape move, as is seen in the performance gap labeled D of Fig. 2.1. If the EA has lost too much diversity, it may be unable to find any areas of improved fitness to exploit.

So what would improve the overall performance of the EA in the dynamic environment? We are looking for techniques that keep the EA fitness from dropping very far at points labeled B, and techniques that increase the slope in regions labeled C.

Diversity maintenance has been the focus of many of the studies of EAs in dynamic environments, most notably the early and much cited research of [14]. Diversity maintenance can help keep the fitness drops at points labeled B from dipping so low, because wherever the global maximum moves, there is population coverage not very far away.

Steepening the slope over area C involves the need to continuously find higher peaks, but also involves rapidly climbing peaks that have been found. Diversity maintenance might help in this area, since the offspring of a diverse population might explore new regions of the search space, enabling the discovery of higher peaks. In multi-modal landscapes, however, diversity could reduce performance in this area, since population members with good fitness that are located on sub-optimal peaks could constantly dilute new generations with low-fitness offspring. Performance improvement in this area reflects the common tradeoff in EA research between exploration for better solutions and refinement of the solutions that have been found. Performance improvement in this area in dynamic environments might require a combination of techniques.

2.4 Algorithm Attributes

Faced with a plethora of possible types of dynamics, for an EA to be successful in a dynamic environment it must be able to accomplish two goals:

1. Detect the change in the landscape.
2. Efficiently respond to the change in the environment.

In this section, we will analyze the problem of dynamic fitness landscapes associated with each of these two activities.

2.4.1 Change Detection

If a fitness landscape changes and there are no members of the EA population in the area of the problem search space that has been changed, the change will go undetected. Since, as an EA operates, the population converges towards a single value, in general, the longer the EA has been operating, the more areas of the problem search space will be unpopulated.

Unfortunately, the population size needed to cover a multi-dimensional search space to assure detection of all possible landscape feature changes is very large. To illustrate this, let us first examine changes to an N-dimensional landscape feature change that is symmetrically detectable in all dimensions within a distance ε of the center of the feature. Stated differently, a landscape feature change will be detected by a population member if the feature center is within an N-dimensional sphere of radius ε of the member, since the volume of an N-dimensional sphere is defined as all of the points in N-space within distance r of the center of the sphere.

Reviewing geometry, the volume of an N-dimensional sphere of radius r is [68]:

$$V = \left(\frac{1}{\left(\frac{N}{2}\right)!}\right) \pi^{\left(\frac{N}{2}\right)} r^N \tag{2.1}$$

when N is even, and:

$$V = \left(\frac{2^{\left(\frac{N+1}{2}\right)}}{N!!}\right) \pi^{\left(\frac{N-1}{2}\right)} r^N \tag{2.2}$$

when N is odd, and where:

$$N! = N(N-1)(N-2)\ldots; \text{ and } N!! = N(N-2)(N-4)\ldots.$$

It should be noted that $V \to 0$ as $N \to \infty$. Therefore, the probability of any specific member of a uniformly distributed population being in a position to detect a symmetric change of size ε in a landscape gets small very fast as dimension increases, and can be expressed as $P_{detect1}$ where:

$$P_{detect1} = \frac{\left(\frac{1}{\left(\frac{N}{2}\right)!}\right) \pi^{\left(\frac{N}{2}\right)} \varepsilon^N}{\prod_{i=1}^{N} \rho_i} \tag{2.3}$$

when N is even, and:

$$P_{detect1} = \frac{\left(\frac{2^{\left(\frac{N+1}{2}\right)}}{N!!}\right) \pi^{\left(\frac{N-1}{2}\right)} \varepsilon^N}{\prod_{i=1}^{N} \rho_i} \tag{2.4}$$

when N is odd, and ρ_n is the range of the search space along each dimension N. It becomes clear that, as N increases, this probability becomes very small very quickly. Therefore, any hope of detection of a landscape change in higher-dimensional spaces is dependent upon the landscape change being detectable in more than a localized volume. In high-dimensional problems, any changes must be detectable over very large ranges in one or more dimensions and there must be members of the population in the areas where the landscape change is detectable, or the landscape change will go undetected.

It is clear, then, that population diversity plays a pivotal role in the detection of fitness landscape changes. The less of the search space the population covers, the less likely that a population member will be within the detectable range of any landscape change.[1]

A number of mechanisms have been implemented by EA researchers to detect changes in a fitness landscape. Most are related to a reduction in the current fitness of the population. These are, at best, only capable of identifying when a previous maximum becomes diminished and are generally incapable of identifying when a new, and better, maximum develops. There are other problems associated with the use of a current reduction in population fitness to identify a change in the fitness landscape that are related to incorrect identification of landscape changes. A description of these problems can be found in [46]. There is no known research regarding the assessment of whether detecting fitness landscape changes is relevant to the performance of the EA. For example, detecting and responding to a small movement of a sub-optimal peak in a remote region of the landscape may not have any bearing on the EA performance, or it may degrade the performance.

2.4.2 Response to Change

Even if a population member is in the area where the fitness landscape change occurs, the stochastic features of the EA do not guarantee that the EA will respond to the change. The first EA action that controls the initial response of the EA is the selection operator. If the population member identifying the environment change is not selected, the fitness information about the change is lost to future EA operations.

2.5 Summary

We have reviewed some of the difficulties that dynamic landscapes present to EAs. We have also provided reasons why the detection of changes in a fitness landscape requires population diversity. Diversity creation and diversity maintenance techniques will be required for EAs to perform well in dynamic environments.

Response, by an EA, to a detected change in the fitness landscape is dependent upon the relationship between the fitness value where the change is detected and fitness of the remainder of the population. Improved response to detected changes in landscapes will require algorithm attributes that change this relationship.

---

[1] It should also be noted that the discussed relationship between search-space size and feature detection also applies to the detection of "interesting regions" and "gradients" in the operation of EAs in static landscapes. In higher dimensions, gradients that will direct the search towards the desired optimum must be detectable from long Euclidean distances in at least one dimension or population sizes must be very large, or both.

3

Solutions from Nature and Engineering

3.1 Overview

With an understanding of the problem at hand from the previous chapter, we will now explore a few of the methods used to deal with this type of problem in nature and in engineering. Biological systems include mechanisms for adapting to changing environments. In engineering, control systems must often be designed to respond properly to unexpected control inputs. This chapter explores a few dynamic adaptation techniques used in biological systems and control engineering to examine opportunities for incorporation of their techniques into EA models and theory.

3.2 Biological Systems

As mentioned before, any EA in a changing environment has to face two specific issues: detection and response. It must be able to detect a change in the landscape, and must be able to respond efficiently to that change. Natural evolution, as first explained by Darwin [16], has been observed to be quite successful in the dynamic environment in which we live. By creating life forms that are adaptable in the face of change, evolution has resulted in the positioning of life forms in some of the most unlikely habitats on the planet. In many cases in nature, however, significant changes in the environment take place at time scales that are several orders of magnitude longer than the time for a single generation of any species adapting to the change [48]. This gives the species time to adapt to the changes through use of a genetic search of possibly advantageous alternatives. When using EAs to solve dynamic problems, however, the environmental change period is often of the order of a few tens of generations, due to computational limitations. Biology offers one specific example of essentially "real-time" genetic adaptation: the immune system. Mechanisms of the immune system that appear to be useful in dealing with dynamic environments will be addressed in this section.

3.2.1 Immunology Background

Organisms have two basic types of immunity: innate immunity and acquired immunity. Innate immunity includes barrier structures, such as external skin and mucous membranes, and standard, memoryless measures such as inflammation. While innate immune responses are useful in avoiding or suppressing changes in the environment, that is generally not what we are interested in accomplishing with an EA. Therefore, innate immunological defense mechanisms will not be further discussed here.

The type of immunity called acquired immunity is much more applicable to our interests. Acquired immunity of the mammalian immune system is distinguished by the following features [21]:

1. Detection and induction – the system detects the presence of an antigen and even previously unseen antigens can induce an immune response.
2. Diversity and specificity – the system can address at least 10^9 antigens, and the response is very specific to each antigen.
3. Memory – the system mounts a faster response to the antigens it has seen before.
4. Self-limitation – the system controls its own reaction and suppresses it when it is no longer needed.

In the area of diversity and specificity for 10^9 antigens, estimates have been made that it would require over 100 million immunoglobulin genes to create the combinations necessary to accomplish this feat, but, in actuality, the human genome has only thousands of genes dedicated to the problem [21].

In 1987 Susumu Tonegawa won the Nobel Prize in Medicine for his discovery of the genetic principle of immune system diversity. Tonegawa showed that the sizes of DNA fragments of immunoglobulin-containing genes differ between embryonic and somatic DNA. Embryonic cells contain the germline immunoglobulin DNA, but when they are stimulated to become a B cell, the DNA segments re-join in a variety of different ways. Antibody diversity results from this recombination during maturation of the cell. This process is called "somatic recombination." The large number of cells, with many different configurations of DNA segments, flood the search space of plausible antigens with what are essentially sensors, capable of detecting specific antigens. In this manner, the presence of an antigen is detected through the interaction with the receptors of pre-existing antigen-specific immune cells. When an antigen is detected, many copies of the associated B cell are made, each one having copies of the selected antigen. This activity is called "clonal proliferation" but it does not make exact copies of the triggered cell. Additional diversity is added through what is called "somatic hypermutation," where the copied cells have a mutation rate several orders of magnitude higher than normal cells [51]. This somatic hypermutation provides the additional diversity necessary to "fine-tune" the selected antibody. Some of these B-cell clones become memory cells and are retained in circulation to provide a more rapid specific response to later detections of the same antigen [21].

3.2.2 Application of Immune System Techniques

The immune system generates and maintains its ability to rapidly adapt to new antigens (which can be viewed as "changes in its environment") through a combination of:

- memory features that retain examples of recent adaptations,
- somatic recombination, which blankets the search space with detectors, and
- somatic hypermutation, which fine tunes the immune system response once an antigen is detected.

It should be noted, however, that a major difference between biological systems and EAs exists that could reduce the applicability, relevance, and usefulness of techniques transferred from biology to EAs. In biological systems, the major energy expense is in reproduction, whereas in most EA applications the major energy expense (i.e., computational resource expense) is in the fitness function evaluation. If one makes the reasonable assumption that energy expenditure is somehow included in the overall evaluation of useful adaptation strategies, then it is possible that discoveries of efficient mechanisms for biological systems may not prove to be efficient for EAs.

3.3 Engineering Control Systems

When a closed sequence of cause-and-effect relationships exists among the variables of a system, this is called feedback. Viewed in this light, an EA can be viewed as a feedback control system that is trying to position the members of the population on the highest peak of a fitness landscape. An EA represented as a control system uses a stochastic search operator (mutation), feedback measurement (fitness evaluation), probabilistic inclusion of the feedback information (selection), and a probabilistic placement refinement technique (crossover). One possible view of an EA as a control system is illustrated as Fig. 3.1.

In this figure, the input signals are the positions of the members of the population at time t, represented as the vector $x(t)$. Without considering the feedback loop, the only control function in the search for optimal member positioning is mutation, which functions as a random search and positioning operator. The feedback loop first involves the sensor operation, which is the fitness function evaluation. This detects the underlying fitness landscape for each of the population members. This sensor information is fed into the feedback control function which executes selection and crossover functions to

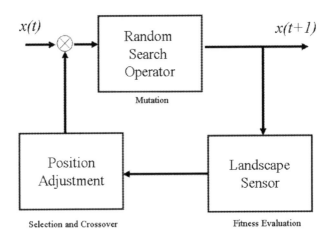

Fig. 3.1. A control system view of an EA

adjust the placement of the population prior to the next execution of the mutation operator. In an EA implementation without crossover, the feedback loop would consist of only the sensor (fitness function evaluation) and the selection operations.

When viewed this way, an EA is a complex, multi-input, multi-output, non-linear system that has resisted significant attempts to perform control system-based analysis and prediction of EA behavior. Although the complexity of the analysis necessary to determine control theory-based behavior predictions of EAs remains currently beyond our grasp, there are control systems that are specifically designed to operate in dynamic environments and it may be fruitful to examine them to determine if there are any useful characteristics of these control systems that might be adapted for EA use.

There is one type of control system that is commonly used to deal with control problems where the control environment is changing. It is called a "sliding mode control" system, which changes its structure and operation depending upon real-time detection of the control problem at hand.

3.3.1 Sliding Mode Control Systems

Sliding mode control systems are designed to operate in varying environments and consist of a suite of feedback control laws combined with a suite of decision rules. The system can be viewed as a combination of several predetermined, fixed control system solutions placed at various points throughout the possible solution space, with each fixed control system to be used in a specific region of the control environment. The decision rules (also called the switching function) are designed to determine which of the individual control systems (or, in complex implementations, which combination of individual control systems) are to be used at any specific time. Switching between individual (usually linear) control systems makes it possible to control high-order, non-linear, variable processes.

The key to successful sliding mode control systems is for the designers to anticipate in which environments the control system will be required to operate, design specific control systems for operation in each environment, and derive switching rules that can identify in which environment the system is operating. This amounts to pre-positioning solutions throughout the solution space and using these solutions at appropriate times. It is of interest to note that. because of the complexity of the individual control systems and the attendant decision rules, EAs have been used in the design of sliding mode control systems [36].

To summarize how this approach relates to the design of EAs for dynamic environments, sliding mode control designers are required to anticipate all of the control system environments to be encountered. They must then prepare a set of control parameters that can perform adequately when the control system is operating in that region of the design space. In an EA implementation, we generally do not know the characteristics of the fitness landscape in advance, but it may be possible to use diversity-creating mechanisms to position predetermined solutions throughout the possible search space to give EAs a head start in quickly adapting to an optimum relocating to any specific area of the search space. With respect to existing EA implementations, this technique would be related to the use of diversity-creating mechanisms to position possible problem solutions in the general area of the problem optima, and also somewhat related to EA implementations where memory is used to position solutions in the search space to permit quick re-adaptation to circumstances seen before.

3.4 Summary

We have seen that both biological system behavior and control system engineering techniques deal with changing environments using diversity-related techniques. The immune system uses techniques that attempt to blanket the search space with coarse detectors which can further refine and direct the immune response when the detectors are triggered. Designers of sliding mode control systems pre-populate regions of the solution space with solutions that perform adequately, and then switch between the solutions as necessary. Both of these techniques appear to have potential use in the design of EAs for dynamic environments.

4

Diversity Measurement

Chapter 1 identified previous EA research in dynamic fitness landscapes where the researchers applied several diversity-increasing techniques, largely following the intuition that a mostly converged population needs to increase its explorative capability to identify a moved optimum. Chapter 2 identified how diversity improves EA performance in dynamic fitness landscapes. Chapter 3 identified examples from biology and engineering where diversity plays a key role in providing satisfactory solutions to dynamic problems. Having established the importance of diversity to the operation of an EA in a dynamic environment, this chapter will address the measurement of population diversity. One of the problems with diversity measurement is that, historically, it has been computationally expensive. The first section of this chapter will address historical methods of measuring diversity, and introduce a mathematical innovation that provides an efficient method for computing the most common population diversity measures. The second section of this chapter will address the shortcomings of the historical measures of diversity as applied to EAs in dynamic fitness landscapes, and will extend the techniques developed in the first section to derive and present a more useful measure of population diversity for dynamic environments called the "dispersion index."

4.1 Efficient Diversity Measurement

4.1.1 Overview

In EAs, the need to efficiently measure population diversity arises in a variety of contexts, including algorithm stopping and re-starting criteria, fitness sharing, and operator adaptation for performance enhancement for dynamic landscapes. The question of when to stop the EA or when to re-start the EA is often based on a measure of population diversity. In fitness-sharing algorithms, population diversity is used as a basis for distributing the fitness credit. The use of EAs for dynamic fitness landscapes requires measures for maintaining population diversity to ensure that the EA can detect and respond to the changes in the landscape.

Diversity measurement has always been important in the study of EAs. Diversity measurement techniques were introduced in the early days of EA exploration to address the recognized problem of "early convergence," a circumstance where the population members become identical before a satisfactory search has been conducted. As EA techniques became more sophisticated, and dynamic problems started to be addressed, the traditional terms and the measures for "diversity" came to also be used as a measure of search-space coverage. Clearly, "not identical" does not the mean the same thing as "well distributed in the search space." In the EA literature, this difference has only occasionally been acknowledged (see, for example, [32]), and, until recently, little work has been done to address the differences [47], [60], [9], [8], [70]. In this chapter we will introduce a computationally efficient method of computing the most common population diversity measures, where the cost of computation increases linearly with population size. We will then extend this computational method to show that it is applicable to non-binary genotypic alphabets. Finally, we will identify and examine shortcomings of the common diversity measurement techniques and leverage our new computational methods to create a new and computationally efficient measurement of diversity that more accurately reflects a population's distribution in the search space.

4.1.2 Background

Historical Measures of Population Diversity

Traditionally, several methods for estimating population diversity have been used. They include diversity measures in both genotypic space and phenotypic space. In phenotypic space, several pair-wise and "column-based" measures (measuring the variation in values for each specific phenotypic feature) are commonly used (e.g., [18]). In real-number optimization problems, phenotypic space diversity measures are often preferred over binary-encoded genotypic measures. This is because, when using genotypic measures, all bit-wise diversity is treated the same, but differences at various bit positions can represent significantly different levels of phenotypic diversity. Despite this logical preference, genotypic measures are much more common in the EA literature. Principal genotypic measures are population entropy (e.g., [42]) and, much more commonly, pair-wise Hamming distance (e.g., [31]). Pair-wise Hamming distance H of P strings of length L is defined as:

$$H = \sum_{j=1}^{j=P-1} \sum_{j'=j+1}^{j'=P} \left(\sum_{i=1}^{i=L} |y_{ij} - y_{ij'}| \right) \tag{4.1}$$

where $y_{ij}, y_{ij'} \in \{0,1\}$ and the generalized notation:

$$\sum_{k=1}^{k=M-1} \sum_{k'=k+1}^{k'=M} f(x_k, x_{k'}), \qquad (4.2)$$

is the sum of the results of the application of $f(x_k, x_{k'})$ to all pair-wise combinations of the members x_k and $x_{k'}$ of a given population of size M. The obvious problem in the practical use of pair-wise population diversity measures is that the computation of the measure is quadratic with the size of the population P for pair-wise selection:

$$\binom{P}{2} = \frac{P^2 - P}{2}. \qquad (4.3)$$

The most commonly used measures of population diversity include pairwise Hamming distance in genotypic space, and column-based pair-wise distance and column variance in phenotypic space. Figures 4.1 through 4.7 provide illustrations of three common diversity measures, using a simple genetic algorithm (GA), a population of 20 on a 2-dimensional, multi-modal landscape similar to that described in [45]. Gray code was used for the binary representation for the GA. Figure 4.1 is the initial population distribution. Figures 4.2 through 4.4 show the convergence of the population at generations 5, 16, and 20 respectively.

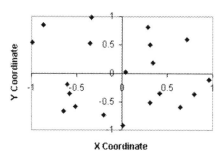

Fig. 4.1. Population at generation=1

Figure 4.5 shows the pair-wise Hamming distance at each generation. Figure 4.6 provides the sum of the pair-wise distances of each column, and Fig. 4.7 provides the sum of the variances of each column.

As can be seen in Fig. 4.3, the population has lost nearly all of its diversity by generation 16. The three diversity measures provide somewhat different views of this loss of diversity, with the column variances (Fig. 4.7) most clearly indicating population convergence, while the low-order bit differences cause the genotypic space pair-wise Hamming distance measure (Fig. 4.5) to indicate more diversity than is present in phenotypic space.

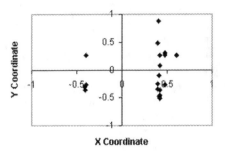

Fig. 4.2. Population at generation=5

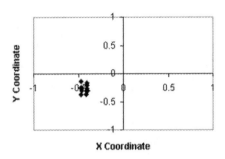

Fig. 4.3. Population at generation=16

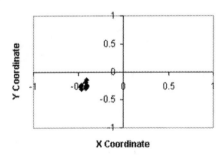

Fig. 4.4. Population at generation=20

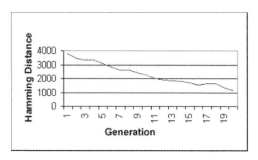

Fig. 4.5. Population pair-wise Hamming distance

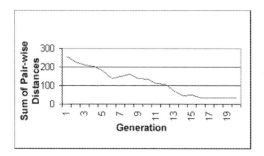

Fig. 4.6. Sum of pair-wise distances

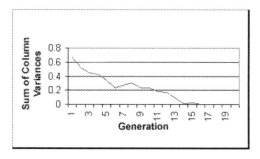

Fig. 4.7. Sum of column variances

4.1.3 Concept Review

The new method for computing common population diversity methods to be presented herein is derived from some traditional engineering concepts that we have adapted to this problem. To facilitate the upcoming discussion, a brief review of these concepts is provided.

The first concept of interest is the centroid. The centroid of an object, also called the center of mass or center of gravity, is the point of balance for the entire object. The coordinates of the centroid are the coordinates of the midpoints of the mass distribution along each axis.

The second concept of interest is the moment of inertia. Moment of inertia is a term used in many engineering problems and calculations. Just as mass is the relationship between force and acceleration according to Newton's second law, moment of inertia is the relationship between torque and angular acceleration. The moment of inertia indicates how easily an object rotates about an axis of rotation. In any object, the parts that are farthest from the axis of rotation contribute more to the moment of inertia than the parts that are closer to the axis. Conceptually, when the axis of rotation goes through the centroid of an object, the moment of inertia is a measure of how far the mass of the object is distributed from the center of gravity of the object. The engineering moment of inertia for a point mass is defined as:

$$I = mr^2 \qquad (4.4)$$

where: I is the usual symbol for moment of inertia, m is the mass, and r^2 is the square of the distance to the axis of rotation.

It should be noticed that, just as there are many possible mass distributions that have the same centroid, there are many possible distributions of mass that will have the same moment of inertia for an axis of rotation. Indeed, the entire mass distribution can be concentrated into one point at a distance from the axis called the *radius of gyration* to generate an identical moment of inertia. It must be noted that this point will have a position in the area that depends not only upon the distribution of the mass, but also on the position of the reference axis. A final concept of importance is that, for a given mass distribution and a coordinate system origin at a point a, the sum of the moments of inertia for any coordinate system with its origin at a is constant.

For the remainder of this chapter we introduce the notation: I_{cx} is the moment of inertia about an axis x which passes through the centroid, I_{ox} is the moment of inertia about an axis x that passes through the origin of the search-space coordinate system, I_C is the sum of the moments of inertia about the distribution centroid, and I_O is the sum of the moments of inertia about the search-space origin.

4.1.4 A New Method of Computing Population Diversity

Our new method of computing population diversity is based on extension of the concept of moment of inertia for measurement of mass distribution into arbitrarily high-dimensionality spaces, and was first described in [47].

Extended into N-space, the coordinates of the centroid of P equally weighted points in N-space, $C = (c_1, c_2, c_3, \ldots, c_N)$, are computed as follows:

$$c_i = \frac{\sum_{j=1}^{j=P} x_{ij}}{P} \qquad (4.5)$$

where $x_{ij} \in \Re$ and c_i is the ith coordinate of the centroid.

Continuing with P equally weighted points in N-space, we define the moment of inertia-based diversity measure as the sum of the moments of inertia about their centroid:

$$I_C = \sum_{i=1}^{i=N} \sum_{j=1}^{j=P} (x_{ij} - c_i)^2. \tag{4.6}$$

As will be shown in later sections, this measurement of population diversity is closely related to commonly used measures of both genotypic diversity and phenotypic diversity, providing a single diversity measurement method for use in both situations. The principal advantage of this measure of diversity is that, in comparison with traditional methods of computing pair-wise population diversity which are quadratic in population size, P, this method is linear in P. Specifically, for an N-dimensional problem with a population size of P, computation of the coordinates of the centroid requires $N \times P$ additions and N divisions. Computation of the moment of inertia around the centroid is then $N \times P$ subtractions plus $N \times P$ multiplications plus $N \times P$ additions. Total computational requirements for the centroid-based moment of inertia, therefore, are $4(NP) + N$ calculations, showing it to be a computationally efficient diversity measure.

4.1.5 Relationship to Diversity Measures in Genotypic Space

Genotypic diversity of EAs is most often measured using pair-wise Hamming distance, but the population diversity is much more efficiently computed using the new moment of inertia method.

When applying the moment of inertia calculation in the context of binary strings, each bit is assumed to be an independent "spatial" dimension. Under these circumstances, the coordinates of the centroid, $(c_1, c_2, c_3, \ldots, c_L)$, of P bit strings of length L are computed as:

$$c_i = \frac{\sum_{j=1}^{j=P} x_{ij}}{P} \tag{4.7}$$

and the sum of moments of inertia about the centroid is:

$$I_C = \sum_{i=1}^{i=L} \sum_{j=1}^{j=P} (x_{ij} - c_i)^2. \tag{4.8}$$

It turns out that by making a transition from *discrete* mathematics to *continuous* mathematics, we can show that the moment of inertia diversity measure, as described in Eq. (4.8), is equal to the pair-wise Hamming distance divided by the population size, and provides a much more computationally efficient method of computing pair-wise Hamming distance.

Theorem 4.1. *For $y_{ij} \in \{0,1\}$:*

$$\sum_{i=1}^{i=L} \sum_{j=1}^{j=P-1} \sum_{j'=j+1}^{j'=P} |y_{ij} - y_{ij'}| = P \left[\sum_{i=1}^{i=L} \sum_{j=1}^{j=P} (y_{ij} - c_i)^2 \right] \qquad (4.9)$$

where:

$$c_i = \frac{\sum_{j=1}^{j=P} x_{ij}}{P}.$$

Verbally, the pair-wise Hamming distance for P bit strings of length L is equal to the sum of the L-space moments of inertia of the population computed around the centroid of the population times the population size. In short, the pair-wise Hamming distance is the binary case of the centroid moment of inertia.

Proof.[1] First we will examine the right hand side of the theorem:

$$P \sum_{i=1}^{L} \sum_{j=1}^{P} (y_{ij} - c_j)^2 = P \sum_{i=1}^{L} \sum_{j=1}^{P} \left(y_{ij} - \frac{\sum_{j=1}^{P} y_{ij}}{P} \right)^2$$

$$= P \sum_{i=1}^{L} \sum_{j=1}^{P} \left(y_{ij}^2 - 2y_{ij} \frac{\sum_{j=1}^{P} y_{ij}}{P} + \frac{1}{P^2} (\sum_{j=1}^{P} y_{ij})^2 \right)$$

$$= P \sum_{i=1}^{L} \left[\sum_{j=1}^{P} y_{ij}^2 - \frac{2}{P} (\sum_{j}^{P} y_{ij})^2 + \frac{1}{P^2} \sum_{j=1}^{P} (\sum_{j=1}^{P} y_{ij})^2 \right]$$

$$= P \sum_{i=1}^{L} \left[\sum_{j=1}^{P} y_{ij}^2 - \frac{2}{P} (\sum_{j=1}^{P} y_{ij})^2 + \frac{1}{P} (\sum_{j=1}^{P} y_{ij})^2 \right]$$

$$= P \sum_{i=1}^{L} \left[\sum_{j=1}^{P} y_{ij}^2 - \frac{1}{P} (\sum_{j=1}^{P} y_{ij})^2 \right] = P \sum_{i=1}^{L} \sum_{j=1}^{P} y_{ij}^2 - \sum_{i=1}^{L} \left(\sum_{j=1}^{P} y_{ij} \right)^2. \qquad (4.10)$$

To examine the left hand side of the theorem, let us first examine the properties of the quantity:

$$\sum_{i=1}^{L} \sum_{j=1}^{P} \sum_{j'=1}^{P} (y_{ij} - y_{ij'})^2 = \sum_{i=1}^{L} \sum_{j=1}^{P} \sum_{j'=1}^{P} y_{ij}^2 - 2 \sum_{i=1}^{L} \sum_{j=1}^{P} \sum_{j'=1}^{P} y_{ij} y_{ij'} + \sum_{i=1}^{L} \sum_{j=1}^{P} \sum_{j'=1}^{P} y_{ij'}^2$$

---

[1] Proof based on suggestions by Chris Reedy, PhD.

$$= 2 \sum_{i=1}^{L} \left[P \sum_{j=1}^{P} y_{ij}^2 - (\sum_{j=1}^{P} y_{ij})^2 \right]. \tag{4.11}$$

Examined differently, and changing the notation for convenience, such that:

$$\sum_{i=1}^{L} \sum_{j=1}^{P-1} \sum_{j'=j+1}^{P} \equiv \sum_{i} \sum_{j} \sum_{j'>j}, \tag{4.12}$$

noticing that:

$$\sum_{i} \sum_{j} \sum_{j'} (y_{ij} - y_{ij'})^2 = \sum_{i} \sum_{j} \sum_{j'<j} (y_{ij} - y_{ij'})^2$$
$$+ \sum_{i} \sum_{j} \sum_{j'=j} (y_{ij} - y_{ij'})^2 + \sum_{i} \sum_{j} \sum_{j'>j} (y_{ij} - y_{ij'})^2 \tag{4.13}$$

and since:

$$\sum_{i} \sum_{j} \sum_{j'=j} (y_{ij} - y_{ij'})^2 = 0 \tag{4.14}$$

then:

$$\sum_{i} \sum_{j} \sum_{j'} (y_{ij} - y_{ij'})^2 = \sum_{i} \sum_{j} \sum_{j'<j} (y_{ij} - y_{ij'})^2 + \sum_{i} \sum_{j} \sum_{j'>j} (y_{ij} - y_{ij'})^2 \tag{4.15}$$

so, by symmetry:

$$\sum_{i} \sum_{j} \sum_{j'} (y_{ij} - y_{ij'})^2 = 2 \sum_{i} \sum_{j} \sum_{j'>j} (y_{ij} - y_{ij'})^2. \tag{4.16}$$

Combining (4.11) and (4.16):

$$2 \sum_{i} \sum_{j} \sum_{j'>j} (y_{ij} - y_{ij'})^2 = 2 \sum_{i} \left[P \sum_{j} y_{ij}^2 - (\sum_{j} y_{ij})^2 \right] \tag{4.17}$$

so:

$$\sum_{i} \sum_{j} \sum_{j'>j} (y_{ij} - y_{ij'})^2 = \sum_{i} \left[P \sum_{j} y_{ij}^2 - (\sum_{j} y_{ij})^2 \right]. \tag{4.18}$$

Since, for $y_{ij} \in \{0,1\}$, the left hand side of the theorem:

$$\sum_{i=1}^{i=L} \sum_{j=1}^{j=P-1} \sum_{j'=j+1}^{j'=P} |y_{ij} - y_{ij'}| = \sum_{i} \sum_{j} \sum_{j'>j} (y_{ij} - y_{ij'})^2, \tag{4.19}$$

combining (4.10), (4.18), and (4.19):

$$\sum_{i} \left[P \sum_{j} y_{ij}^2 - (\sum_{j} y_{ij})^2 \right] = P \sum_{i} \sum_{j} y_{ij}^2 - \sum_{i} \left(\sum_{j} y_{ij} \right)^2 \tag{4.20}$$

shows that the pair-wise Hamming distance is equal to the sum of the moments of inertia around the centroid times the population size. □

4.1.6 Explanation and Example

The moment of inertia method for computing pair-wise Hamming distance works because all coordinates are either 0 or 1. This means that $x^2 = x$ and x times x' is equal to x or x', or both. As a simplified example of how this computational method is used, consider a population of six strings ($P = 6$), each three bits long and having values $y_{gene,individual}$ equal to:

$$y_{11} = 1, y_{21} = 1, y_{31} = 1$$

$$y_{12} = 0, y_{22} = 0, y_{32} = 0$$

$$y_{13} = 1, y_{23} = 1, y_{33} = 0$$

$$y_{14} = 1, y_{24} = 0, y_{34} = 0$$

$$y_{15} = 0, y_{25} = 1, y_{35} = 0$$

$$y_{16} = 1, y_{26} = 0, y_{36} = 1.$$

The coordinates of the population centroid are:

$$C_1 = \frac{4}{6} = \frac{2}{3}, \; C_2 = \frac{3}{6} = \frac{1}{2}, \; C_3 = \frac{2}{6} = \frac{1}{3}.$$

The population size times the sum of the moments of inertia around the centroid:

$$P \left[\sum_{i=1}^{i=L} \sum_{j=1}^{j=P} (y_{ij} - c_i)^2 \right] \tag{4.21}$$

is computed as:

$$6 \left[\left(1 - \frac{2}{3}\right)^2 + \left(0 - \frac{2}{3}\right)^2 + \left(1 - \frac{2}{3}\right)^2 + \left(1 - \frac{2}{3}\right)^2 + \left(0 - \frac{2}{3}\right)^2 + \left(1 - \frac{2}{3}\right)^2 \right]$$

$$+6 \left[\left(1 - \frac{1}{2}\right)^2 + \left(0 - \frac{1}{2}\right)^2 + \left(1 - \frac{1}{2}\right)^2 + \left(0 - \frac{1}{2}\right)^2 + \left(1 - \frac{1}{2}\right)^2 + \left(0 - \frac{1}{2}\right)^2 \right]$$

$$+6 \left[\left(1 - \frac{1}{3}\right)^2 + \left(0 - \frac{1}{3}\right)^2 + \left(0 - \frac{1}{3}\right)^2 + \left(0 - \frac{1}{3}\right)^2 + \left(0 - \frac{1}{3}\right)^2 + \left(1 - \frac{1}{3}\right)^2 \right]$$

$$= 6 \left(\frac{12}{9} + \frac{6}{4} + \frac{12}{9} \right) = (8 + 9 + 8) = 25$$

which is the same value as the pair-wise Hamming distance for this population.

4.1.7 Computational Efficiency

The computational efficiency of the moment of inertia method of computing pair-wise Hamming distance makes a considerable difference at population sizes normally encountered in evolutionary computation. For a bit string
length of 50 and a population size of 1000, the number of computations necessary for calculation of the pair-wise Hamming distance by the moment of
inertia method is two orders of magnitude less than that required by the usual
computational methods. Even adjusting for the fact that the moment of inertia method involves floating-point calculations, whereas Hamming distance
calculations can be made using integer or binary data types, the moment
of inertia method for computing pair-wise Hamming distance is considerably
more efficient.

4.1.8 An Alternative Diversity Computation Method for Binary Genotypic Space

In this section we develop an even more efficient method for computing the
pair-wise Hamming distance for a binary population than the one provided
above. While computationally very efficient, the following method is useful
for determining the overall population diversity for a set of binary strings,
but, since the individual string diversity contribution is not computed as an
intermediate step, it is not as useful as the previous method for determining
the population diversity contribution of any individual string.

Theorem 4.2. *For $y_{ij} \in \{0,1\}$:*

$$\sum_{i=1}^{i=L} \sum_{j=1}^{j=P} \sum_{j'=j+1}^{j'=P} |y_{ij} - y_{ij'}| = \sum_{i=1}^{L} k_i(P - k_i) \tag{4.22}$$

where k_i is the number of ones in column i:

$$k_i = \sum_{j=1}^{P} y_{ij}. \tag{4.23}$$

Proof. For any particular "column" i in the population, the number of pair-
wise combinations is:

$$\binom{P}{2} = \frac{P(P-1)}{2}. \tag{4.24}$$

If there are k_i ones in column i, the number of pair-wise combinations of these
ones is:

$$\binom{k_i}{2} = \frac{k_i(k_i - 1)}{2}. \tag{4.25}$$

If there are k_i ones in column i, then there are $P - k_i$ zeros in the column. The number of pair-wise combinations of these zeros is:

$$\binom{P - k_i}{2} = \frac{(P - k_i)(P - k_i - 1)}{2}. \tag{4.26}$$

Since pair-wise Hamming distance is the sum of the column-wise combinations that do not pair a one with a one or a zero with a zero:

$$\sum_{i=1}^{i=L} \sum_{j=1}^{j=P} \sum_{j'=j+1}^{j'=P} |y_{ij} - y_{ij'}|$$

$$= \sum_{i=1}^{L} \left[\frac{P(P-1)}{2} - \frac{k_i(k_i - 1)}{2} - \frac{(P - k_i)(P - k_1 - 1)}{2} \right]$$

$$= \sum_{i=1}^{i=L} \frac{1}{2} \left[P^2 - P - k_i^2 + k_i - P^2 + Pk_i + P + Pk_i - k_i^2 - k_i \right]$$

$$= \frac{1}{2} \sum_{i=1}^{L} (2k_i P - 2k_i^2) = \sum_{i=1}^{L} k_i(P - k_i). \quad \square \tag{4.27}$$

This method of computing the pair-wise Hamming distance of a binary string population is linear in P and can be performed in integer arithmetic. However, as pointed out earlier, it is not convenient for ascertaining the individual diversity contribution of specific population members.

4.1.9 Computing Diversity Measures in Phenotypic Space

For an individual dimension, the moment of inertia diversity measure is closely related to the calculation of statistical variance:

$$\sigma^2 = \frac{\sum (X - \mu)^2}{N} \tag{4.28}$$

differing only in the use of population size in the calculation.

The moment of inertia diversity measure calculation, when applied in phenotypic space with real-numbered parameters, is closely related to the sum of the column variances. It should be noted, however, that when using the moment of inertia population diversity calculation method for real-numbered parameters, just as when combining traditional column-wise phenotypic diversity measures across columns, attention must be paid to individual parameter scaling. When searching a space, it is important to realize the impact of search-space size on the problem to be solved, and understand the resolution (granularity) with which the search for a solution is to be conducted. For example, in a real-numbered convex-space optimization problem, the search space is defined by the ranges of the real-numbered parameters. If the range of parameter A is twice as large as that of parameter B, at the same granularity of search, the search space is twice as large along dimension A as along dimension B. In different cases the resolution of interest might be defined as a single percentage of the range, and this percentage might be equally applicable to all parameters. In this case, all parameters should be scaled equally. The moment of inertia calculations can be transformed to equally scale all parameters merely by dividing all parameter values by the parameter range. As long as the parameters are scaled so that they have an equal granularity of interest, the moment of inertia calculations provide an efficient method for measuring population diversity.

It is possible to envision circumstances where it would be desirable to compare the diversity of two different-sized populations on the same problem. In these cases, scaling the diversity by the population size would then be appropriate. When scaled in this manner, the moment of inertia diversity measure for the real parameter problem is equal to the sum of the column-wise variances of the individual parameters.

Figure 4.8 shows the moment of inertia diversity measure for the example problem used for Figs. 4.1 through 4.7. Comparing Fig. 4.8 to Fig. 4.6 illustrates that, in addition to being more computationally efficient than the pair-wise column distance measure, the moment of inertia measure more dramatically portrays the population loss of diversity by generation 16 than does the pair-wise distance measure.

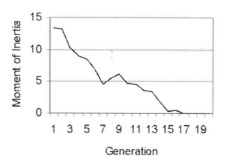

Fig. 4.8. Moment of inertia diversity

4.1.10 Measuring Genotypic Diversity of Non-binary Populations

The primary focus of the research in this book is on binary populations in genotypic space and real-numbered parameters in phenotypic space, but the moment of inertia population diversity measurement can be extended to provide an efficient measure of diversity when using non-binary alphabets for genotypic representation. This extension is provided herein to assist researchers working with non-binary representations.

Recalling that the moment of inertia diversity is computed as:

$$I = mr^2 = \sum_{i=1}^{i=N} \sum_{j=1}^{j=P} (x_{ij} - c_i)^2,$$

we can see that we need to define the centroid, c_i, and the distance from the centroid, $(x_{ij} - c_i)$, for this new situation.

The centroid in this situation is computed using the same spatial measurement techniques that were used for binary populations, extended from two dimensions into the number of orthogonal dimensions necessary to accommodate the size of the non-binary alphabet. Consider an alphabet $\mathbf{A}$ consisting of $|\mathbf{A}|$ different values, a population of size P, and a fixed string length of L. Allele values are now values from the alphabet, $x_{ij} \in \mathbf{A}$. The centroid value for any column, c_j, is now computed as the spatial center of mass of the values of the column.

As a simple example, consider a single column of a population of six members using a trinary alphabet $\mathbf{A} = \{A, B, C\}$. Assume that there are one A, three Bs, and two Cs in the column under consideration. With one-sixth of the mass at the point A, three-sixths of the mass at point B, and two-sixths of the mass at point C, the coordinates of the centroid of this column j are:

$$c_j = \left\{ \frac{1}{6}, \frac{1}{2}, \frac{1}{3} \right\}$$

This example is shown as Fig. 4.9.

Continuing with this example, the distance to the centroid, $(x_{ij} - c_i)$, is computed as follows:

$$\text{if } x_{ij} = A, (x_{ij} - c_i) = D_A = \sqrt{\left(1 - \frac{1}{6}\right)^2 + \left(\frac{1}{2}\right)^2 + \left(\frac{1}{3}\right)^2}$$

$$\text{if } x_{ij} = B, (x_{ij} - c_i) = D_B = \sqrt{\left(\frac{1}{6}\right)^2 + \left(1 - \frac{1}{2}\right)^2 + \left(\frac{1}{3}\right)^2}$$

$$\text{if } x_{ij} = C, (x_{ij} - c_i) = D_C = \sqrt{\left(\frac{1}{6}\right)^2 + \left(\frac{1}{2}\right)^2 + \left(1 - \frac{1}{3}\right)^2}.$$

In general, then, the centroid coordinates in $\mathbf{A}$-space of size z, for column allele position j, are:

$$c_j = \left\{ \frac{\#a_1}{P}, \frac{\#a_2}{P}, \dots, \frac{\#a_z}{P} \right\} \qquad (4.29)$$

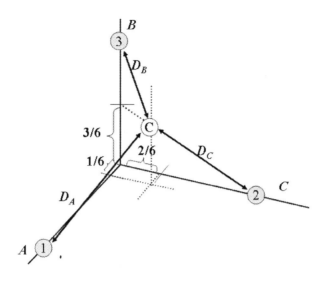

Fig. 4.9. The location of the centroid for an alphabet of three characters

where: $\#a_b$ is the number of times that $x_{ij} = a_b$ in column j.

The distance-squared measure is:

$$(x_{ij} - c_i)^2 = \begin{cases} \text{if } x_{ij} = a_1, (1 - \frac{\#a_1}{P})^2 + (\frac{\#a_2}{P})^2 + \ldots + (\frac{\#a_z}{P})^2 \\ \text{if } x_{ij} = a_2, (\frac{\#a_1}{P})^2 + (1 - \frac{\#a_2}{P})^2 + \ldots + (\frac{\#a_z}{P})^2 \\ \vdots \\ \text{if } x_{ij} = a_z, (\frac{\#a_1}{P})^2 + (\frac{\#a_2}{P})^2 + \ldots + (1 - \frac{\#a_z}{P})^2. \end{cases} \quad (4.30)$$

Using this method, the column-wise square of the distances from the mean column value can be computed. Summing these across the string length L and population P will compute the moment of inertia diversity measure for non-binary alphabet strings.

Let us do this with one final example, comparing a population of six ($P = 6$) short ($L = 4$) DNA fragments ($\mathbf{A} = \{A, C, T, G\}$), having values $y_{gene,individual}$ equal to:

$$y_{11} = A, y_{21} = T, y_{31} = T, y_{41} = C$$

$$y_{12} = C, y_{22} = T, y_{32} = A, y_{42} = T$$

$$y_{13} = T, y_{23} = G, y_{33} = T, y_{43} = C$$

$$y_{14} = G, y_{24} = G, y_{34} = G, y_{44} = G$$
$$y_{15} = A, y_{25} = C, y_{35} = G, y_{45} = G$$
$$y_{16} = T, y_{26} = C, y_{36} = A, y_{46} = G.$$

The coordinates of the population centroid are:

$$C_1 = \{C_{1,A}, C_{1,C}, C_{1,T}, C_{1,G}\} = \left\{\frac{1}{3}, \frac{1}{6}, \frac{1}{3}, \frac{1}{6}\right\}$$

$$C_2 = \{C_{2,A}, C_{2,C}, C_{2,T}, C_{2,G}\} = \left\{0, \frac{1}{3}, \frac{1}{3}, \frac{1}{3}\right\}$$

$$C_3 = \{C_{3,A}, C_{3,C}, C_{3,T}, C_{3,G}\} = \left\{\frac{1}{3}, 0, \frac{1}{3}, \frac{1}{3}\right\}$$

$$C_4 = \{C_{4,A}, C_{4,C}, C_{4,T}, C_{4,G}\} = \left\{0, \frac{1}{3}, \frac{1}{6}, \frac{1}{2}\right\}.$$

The sum of the moments of inertia around the centroid is computed as:

$$I_c = \sum_{i=1}^{i=L} \sum_{j=1}^{j=P} (y_{ij} - c_i)^2$$

$$= 2\left[\left(1-\frac{1}{3}\right)^2 + \left(\frac{1}{6}\right)^2 + \left(\frac{1}{3}\right)^2 + \left(\frac{1}{6}\right)^2\right]$$

$$+ \left[\left(\frac{1}{3}\right)^2 + \left(1-\frac{1}{6}\right)^2 + \left(\frac{1}{3}\right)^2 + \left(\frac{1}{6}\right)^2\right]$$

$$+ 2\left[\left(\frac{1}{3}\right)^2 + \left(\frac{1}{6}\right)^2 + \left(1-\frac{1}{3}\right)^2 + \left(\frac{1}{6}\right)^2\right]$$

$$+ \left[\left(1-\frac{1}{3}\right)^2 + \left(\frac{1}{6}\right)^2 + \left(\frac{1}{3}\right)^2 + \left(1-\frac{1}{6}\right)^2\right]$$

$$+ 2\left[\left(1-\frac{1}{3}\right)^2 + \left(\frac{1}{3}\right)^2 + \left(\frac{1}{3}\right)^2\right] + 2\left[\left(\frac{1}{3}\right)^2 + \left(1-\frac{1}{3}\right)^2 + \left(\frac{1}{3}\right)^2\right]$$

$$+ 2\left[\left(\frac{1}{3}\right)^2 + \left(\frac{1}{3}\right)^2 + \left(1-\frac{1}{3}\right)^2\right] + 2\left[\left(1-\frac{1}{3}\right)^2 + \left(\frac{1}{3}\right)^2 + \left(\frac{1}{3}\right)^2\right]$$

$$+ 2\left[\left(\frac{1}{3}\right)^2 + \left(1-\frac{1}{3}\right)^2 + \left(\frac{1}{3}\right)^2\right] + 2\left[\left(\frac{1}{3}\right)^2 + \left(\frac{1}{3}\right)^2 + \left(1-\frac{1}{3}\right)^2\right]$$

$$+2\left[\left(1-\frac{1}{3}\right)^2+\left(\frac{1}{6}\right)^2+\left(\frac{1}{2}\right)^2\right]+\left[\left(\frac{1}{3}\right)^2+\left(1-\frac{1}{6}\right)^2+\left(\frac{1}{2}\right)^2\right]$$

$$+3\left[\left(\frac{1}{3}\right)^2+\left(\frac{1}{6}\right)^2+\left(1-\frac{1}{2}\right)^2\right]=20.75.$$

For comparison, the less diverse population:

$$y_{11}=A, y_{21}=T, y_{31}=T, y_{41}=T$$
$$y_{12}=A, y_{22}=T, y_{32}=T, y_{42}=A$$
$$y_{13}=G, y_{23}=G, y_{33}=G, y_{43}=G$$
$$y_{14}=G, y_{24}=G, y_{34}=G, y_{44}=G$$
$$y_{15}=T, y_{25}=T, y_{35}=T, y_{45}=A$$
$$y_{16}=A, y_{26}=T, y_{36}=T, y_{46}=G$$

results in coordinates for the population centroid of:

$$C_1=\{C_{1,A},C_{1,C},C_{1,T},C_{1,G}\}=\left\{\frac{1}{2},0,\frac{1}{6},\frac{1}{3}\right\}$$

$$C_2=\{C_{2,A},C_{2,C},C_{2,T},C_{2,G}\}=\left\{0,0,\frac{2}{3},\frac{1}{3}\right\}$$

$$C_3=\{C_{3,A},C_{3,C},C_{3,T},C_{3,G}\}=\left\{0,0,\frac{2}{3},\frac{1}{3}\right\}$$

$$C_4=\{C_{4,A},C_{4,C},C_{4,T},C_{4,G}\}=\left\{\frac{1}{3},0,\frac{1}{6},\frac{1}{2}\right\},$$

and the resultant sum of the moments of inertia for this population is: $I_c=18.61$.

4.1.11 Section Summary

In this section we have introduced a new moment of inertia method for easily computing the most commonly used population diversity measures for real-parameter populations and binary populations. In the case of binary populations, two novel and computationally efficient methods for computing the pair-wise Hamming distance have been presented. The new method of computing these diversity measures has been extended to non-binary alphabets. For larger alphabets, the size of the alphabet increases the complexity of the moment of inertia calculations, but the increase is only linear in alphabet size.

4.2 Improved Diversity Measurement for Dynamic Problems

The contribution of this section will be to address the shortcomings of the current population diversity measures. We will do this by first examining the extent to which the common diversity measures fail to measure search-space coverage, and then provide a new and computationally efficient method for better approximating search-space coverage through an extension of our diversity measurement methods provided in the previous sections.

4.2.1 Limitations of Current Diversity Measurement Methods

As previously mentioned, diversity measurement techniques commonly in use were intended to address the problem of "early convergence." Continued use of these same measures with dynamic problems, where the desired measure is an indicator of search-space coverage, is inappropriate. All of the common population diversity measures in use by the EA community approximate the multi-dimensional property of diversity using a single dimensional measure. These common diversity metrics identify differences between population members, but this does not actually measure the distribution of the population throughout the search space. As mentioned earlier, "not identical" does not mean the same thing as "well distributed in the search space." For each of the common measures, there are many population distributions that will arrive at the same diversity value, but have widely different coverage of the search space. This is most obvious in the case of population entropy:

$$H = \sum \frac{p_i}{P} \log \left(\frac{p_i}{P} \right) \qquad (4.31)$$

where: p_i is the current abundance of a specific genotype and P is the total number of strings in the population. In this case, entropy is maximized if all the strings are different, regardless of their distribution throughout the search space. All the strings could be very closely clustered in a small section of the search space, yet have maximum entropy. In the case of pair-wise Hamming distance, dividing the population into just a few locations in the search space is often sufficient to generate a large value for diversity. As an example of this, notice that pair-wise Hamming distance is maximized by a population that consists entirely of strings that are all ones or all zeros, if the proportion of the one-strings to the zero-strings is 0.5. When using the pair-wise Hamming distance as a diversity measure in genotypic space, for any specific value of Hamming distance, the number of alternate populations with the same pair-wise Hamming distance, Q, is bounded by:

$$Q \leq \left(\frac{P}{2} \right) L \qquad (4.32)$$

for a population size P and binary string length L. Clearly, pair-wise Hamming distance says little about actual coverage of the search space.

Similarly, in phenotypic space, widely separated clusters of population members will generally have a higher moment of inertia than a more evenly dispersed population of the same size. There are many population distributions that will have the same moments of inertia but have widely different search-space coverage.

This can be misleading. When we are using diversity measurement to identify an EA's ability to detect fitness landscape changes throughout the search space, it is important that our diversity measures provide a reliable indication of search-space coverage. Even the most recent research in diversity measures focuses on the differences between population members, and does not address search-space coverage [9], [70].

Search-space coverage is closely related to the mathematical concepts of "dispersion" and "discrepancy" [19]. Our next contribution in this chapter is to build upon our new methods of computing diversity and combine them with mathematical research in discrepancy theory to provide a new, computationally efficient search-space-based diversity measurement, which more accurately measures the uniformity of a population's dispersion through a search space. We will call this new measure the dispersion index, and abbreviate it Δ.

4.2.2 Measurement of Search-Space Coverage

We have already described the methods for improving the computational efficiency of the commonly used diversity measures, but have shown these measures to be incomplete and potentially misleading with respect to search-space coverage. What we will do in this section is introduce two enhancements to the moment of inertia diversity calculations to more completely measure search-space coverage and reduce the potential for misleading measurements.

Discrepancy measurement is the preferred mathematical method for determining the uniformity of search-space coverage, so we will provide some insight into discrepancy theory here.

Discrepancy measurement involves concepts that are loosely based on the same ideas as the Kolomogorov–Smirnov (K–S) test when it is used to compare a distribution of points to the uniform distribution. Reviewing the K–S test, in one dimension the K–S test compares an ordered set of P points X_i to a continuous distribution by computing the difference between the discrete cumulative distribution of the points and the cumulative distribution of the desired continuous distribution. A test statistic D is computed:

$$D = \sup_{1 \le i \le P} \left| F(X_i) - \frac{i}{P} \right|. \tag{4.33}$$

The hypothesis regarding the distributed form of the points is rejected if the test statistic, D, is greater than the critical value obtained from a table.

Unfortunately, the cumulative probability distribution is not well defined in more than one dimension, although an extension to two dimensions, originally for use in astronomy, has been made using the integrated probability in each of the four natural quadrants around a given point [53]. It has also been extended to binned data for two dimensions [61].

For higher dimensions the common measure of uniformity is discrepancy. While not providing a test statistic for uniformity, discrepancy can be used to compare sequences of points in N-space to determine which sequence is more uniform. Discrepancy measures consider the N-dimensional $\Re^N$ space modulo 1 or, equivalently, the N-dimensional torus $T^N = \Re^N / \mathcal{Z}^N$. Instead of identifying the largest difference between cumulative distributions of points and the desired distribution, as the K–S test does, discrepancy identifies the largest difference between the proportion of points included in an N-dimensional space partition and the proportion of the total volume (Lebesgue measure) included in that partition, over all possible space partitions. More formally (and using mostly the notation of [19]), let $J = [a_1, b_1] \times \ldots \times [a_N, b_N] \subseteq \Re^N$ be an interval (parallelepiped, with the sides parallel to the axes) in the N-dimensional space $\Re^N$ with $0 \leq b_i - a_i \leq 1, i = 1, \ldots, N$. Then, in modulo 1, $I = J / \mathcal{Z}^N$ is an interval of the torus T^N. The N-dimensional volume of the interval I is given as:

$$\lambda_N = \prod_{i=1}^{N} (b_i - a_i). \qquad (4.34)$$

Then, for an interval $I \subseteq \Re^N / \mathcal{Z}^N$, and a sequence $(x_p)_{p \geq 1}, x_p \subseteq \Re^N$, let $A(I, P, x_p)$ be the number of points $x_p, 1 \leq p \leq P$, for which $x_p \in I$:

$$A(I, P, x_p) = \sum_{p=1}^{P} \chi_I(\{x_p\}), \qquad (4.35)$$

where: χ_I is the characteristic function of I.

With these definitions, the discrepancy of a sequence of P points in N-dimensional space is defined as:

$$\mathbb{D}_P(x_P) = \sup_{I \subseteq T^N} \left| \frac{A(I, P, x_P)}{P} - \lambda_N(I) \right|. \qquad (4.36)$$

Discrepancy, as defined above, is useful for comparing the uniformity sequences, because, as elaborated in [19], a sequence is uniformly distributed modulo 1 if and only if:

$$\lim_{P \to \infty} \mathbb{D}_P(x_P) = 0. \qquad (4.37)$$

As the mathematically preferred method for computing the uniformity of points in an N-dimensional space, discrepancy provides some insights to useful diversity measurement methods that we will borrow from in later paragraphs. However, calculation of the discrepancy value is far too computationally expensive to be practically employed in most EA solutions.

4.2.3 Dispersion Index, Δ, Defined

As we develop our improved diversity measure, the first key concept that we will employ involves the quantitative assessment of the spread of the points about their centroid. As was mentioned earlier, apparent uniformity in lower-dimensional projections of higher-dimensional space does not guarantee uniformity in the higher-dimensional space. Higher-dimensional spatial distribution uniformity will, however, guarantee that lower-dimensional projections will be uniform. This means that if a population is uniformly distributed in the search space, the moments of inertia I_{cx} for the individual spatial axes through the centroid will be the same as those of a uniform distribution. Since moments of inertia can be either higher or lower than those of uniformly distributed points, the first component of our new diversity measure will compare the individual axis moment of inertia measurements through the centroid to those we would expect were our population actually uniformly distributed. As addressed earlier, the calculation of these moments is computationally efficient. The trick, then, is to compute the moments around the axes for a uniformly distributed population of identical size.

To examine this problem, let us work with an N-dimensional unit cube, but examine only one dimension, since the measurement for all axes will be identical. We will employ the following definition of uniform.

Definition: A population of P points is uniformly distributed across a 1-dimensional interval, I, if they are placed at coordinates U such that:

$$U = \left\{ \frac{I}{P+1}, \frac{2I}{P+1}, \frac{3I}{P+1}, \ldots, \frac{PI}{P+1} \right\}. \tag{4.38}$$

We will then need to compute the moment of inertia for this set of points, but we first need to mention that once a moment of inertia of a set of points, P, is computed for an individual axis, it is easily transformed to the moment of inertial around any parallel axis a distance d from the axis of measurement by adding the value Pd^2. It is trivial to show that, for example, the moment of inertia of the uniformly distributed points described by the previous equation on the unit interval has a centroid coordinate of $c = 0.5$ and that the moment of inertia around the origin is related to the moment of inertia around the centroid by the following equation (dropping the coordinate subscripts, since it is a 1-dimensional distribution):

$$I_o = I_c + Pc^2. \tag{4.39}$$

Now we must compute the moment of inertia of the uniform distribution described above. For convenience, we will compute it about the origin, on a unit interval, and label it I_{Uo}:

$$I_{Uo} = \sum_{n=1}^{P} \left(\frac{n}{P+1} \right)^2. \tag{4.40}$$

As $P \to \infty$, this series converges to $\frac{1}{3}P$, but, unfortunately, usually not fast enough for our purposes.[2] It is easily computed off line, however, and a partial lookup table of values for the 1-dimensional moment of inertia about the origin, divided by the population size, is provided in Table 4.1.

Table 4.1. Uniform distribution moment of inertia from origin divided by population size

P	I_o/P	P	I_o/P
1	0.250000	30	0.327957
2	0.277778	40	0.329268
3	0.291667	50	0.330065
4	0.300000	60	0.330601
5	0.305556	70	0.330986
6	0.309524	80	0.331276
7	0.312500	90	0.331502
8	0.314815	100	0.331683
9	0.316667	150	0.332230
10	0.318182	200	0.332504
11	0.319444	250	0.332669
12	0.320513	300	0.332780
13	0.321429	350	0.332858
14	0.322222	400	0.332918
15	0.322917	500	0.333001
16	0.323529	600	0.333056
17	0.324074	700	0.333096
18	0.324561	800	0.333125
19	0.325000	900	0.333148
20	0.325397	1000	0.333167

The first intermediate component in our calculation of the dispersion index in N-dimensional space is $\mathbb{S}_1$, which compares the individual axis moments of inertia, adjusted to be computed from the origin, to what the origin moment of inertia would be if the distribution were uniform:

$$\mathbb{S}_1 = \max_j \frac{\left[|I_{Uoj} - (I_{cj} + Pc_j^2)|\right]}{P}, \tag{4.41}$$

for $j \in N$, and where I_{Uoj} is the moment of inertia of a uniform distribution of P points in dimension j computed from the origin. Notice that, included in this component, is a measurement of the displacement of the centroid of the points from where it should be for a uniform distribution. For a completely uniform distribution of points, the value of $\mathbb{S}_1$ is zero. Values for $\mathbb{S}_1$ increase with less uniformity.

---

[2] As $P \to \infty$, $I_{Uo} = P \int_0^1 x^2 dx = P\frac{1}{3}x^3|_0^1$.

As shown in Table 4.1, $\frac{1}{4}P \leq I_{oU} \leq \frac{1}{3}P$. From the definition of the moment of inertia measure, the possible values of the moment of inertia around the origin on the unit interval are: $0 \leq I_{ox} \leq P$. Therefore, $0 \leq \mathbb{S}_1 \leq \frac{3}{4}$, and the first component of our dispersion index is $\Delta_1 = 0.75 - \mathbb{S}_1$, which varies from 0 to 0.75, with increasing values indicating better dispersion.

Δ_1 compares the individual dimension spatial spread of the points to the ideal spread of the points. Uniformly distributed individual dimension projections, however, do not guarantee uniform distribution in higher dimensions. So the question becomes, "under what circumstances could a distribution have a large value for Δ_1, yet not be uniform?" The answer lies in the diagonal of the search space.

Populations that have too much or too little of their population distributed along the main diagonal of the search space are the distributions that can be inappropriately given a good or bad dispersion measured using Δ_1 alone. The Hamming distance example cited earlier involving strings of all ones and all zeros is a genotypic example of this diagonal problem. Less obvious are populations that have empty areas along the spatial diagonals. Figures 4.10 and 4.11 provide two examples of population distributions where Δ_1 would indicate a more uniform distribution than is actually present. The distributions in Figs. 4.10 and 4.11 both have Δ_1 values of 0.748. For reference, the much more uniform distribution in Fig. 4.12 has a Δ_1 value of 0.731, and the randomly placed 50 points in Fig. 4.13 have a Δ_1 value of 0.688. Clearly, the $\mathbb{S}_1$ values for Figs. 4.10 and 4.11 indicate a significantly more uniform distribution that is actually present. The point is that if a non-uniformity is along the diagonal of the search space, it will go undetected by Δ_1, since Δ_1 only measures the uniformity of individual dimension projections.

To address this problem we will now develop the second intermediate component of Δ, called Δ_2, which examines the diagonal. Recall that discrepancy theory compares the number of points in volume measures to the number of points that should be there according to the target distribution. While discrepancy theory requires that all possible spatial intervals be considered (thus making the calculation too computationally expensive for our purposes), we are interested in detecting the extent to which we may have been misled by our moment of inertia calculations represented in Δ_1 which, at this point, only includes non-uniformity along the principal diagonal of the search space. In practice, we can accomplish this by sampling only a few of the possible spatial partitions. This examination is further simplified by the fact that Δ_1 will identify population non-uniformities where the population centroid is significantly different than the search-space centroid. Therefore, for our following examination we can use the population centroid as an approximation of the search-space centroid.

If we partition the search space parallel to the axes at the coordinates of the population centroid, the space is partitioned into 2^N partitions. Each partition represents a segment of space representing the points with coordinates either above or below the centroid coordinate for each dimension. Spatial

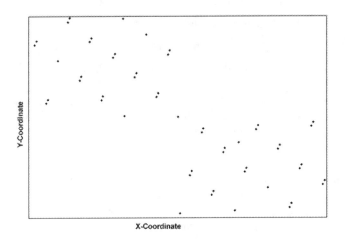

Fig. 4.10. Example of 50 points deceptive to the Δ_1 measure

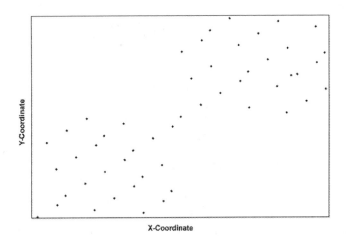

Fig. 4.11. Second example of 50 points deceptive to the Δ_1 measure

partitions represent all pair-wise combinations of the two values for each dimension. When the population centroid is close to the search-space centroid, the diagonal of the search space is contained in two of these partitions. The first is where all points have coordinates that are less than the centroid in all dimensions. The second partition is where all of the points have coordinates that are greater than the centroid in all dimensions. By examining just these two partitions, which can be done with reasonable computational efficiency,

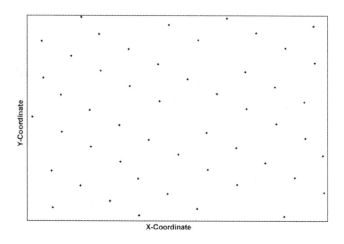

Fig. 4.12. Example of 50 uniformly distributed points

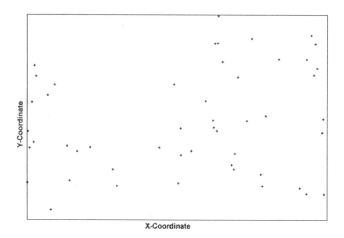

Fig. 4.13. Example of 50 randomly distributed points

we can, in practice, reduce the possibility of mis-classifying the uniformity of
a distribution to negligible levels.

The examination of the two partitions is based on the ideas of discrepancy
theory, and compares the proportion of points in a partition of the search-space
volume to the proportion of the total volume contained in that partition. This
concept must be modified, however, to again accommodate the fact that we
are primarily interested in a relatively few points in multi-dimensional space.
In this environment, the problem inaccuracies caused by comparing a small
integer number of points to a real-number space volume can be significant.
This consideration prevents us from naively dividing the proportion of the
population by the proportion of the search-space volume, as discrepancy theory would do. Instead, we must compare the integer number of points to an
equivalent integer representation of the portion of the search-space volume.
Formally, let $c-$ be the subset of points where the coordinates in all dimensions are less than the population centroid coordinate in the dimension, and
$c+$ be the subset of the points where the coordinates in all dimensions are
greater than the centroid coordinate in the dimension. Then:

$$
\mathbb{S}_2 = \max\left[\frac{\left|\sum_P \chi_{c+} - \text{INT}\left[\left(\frac{\Pi_j(1-c_j)}{\Pi_j \rho_j}\right)P\right]\right|}{P}, \frac{\left|\sum_P \chi_{c-} - \text{INT}\left[\left(\frac{\Pi_j c_j}{\Pi_j \rho_j}\right)P\right]\right|}{P}\right],
$$

$$(4.42)$$

where:

χ_{c-} is the characteristic function of the set of points where all coordinates
i are less than the centroid value for that coordinate;

χ_{c+} is the characteristic function of the set of points where all coordinates
i are greater than the centroid value for that coordinate;

ρ_j is the range of the search space in dimension $j \in N$, so that $\prod_{i=1}^N \rho_j = 1$
for an N-dimensional unit volume; and

$\text{INT}(x)$ is the nearest integer to $x \in \mathfrak{R}$.

Since $0 \leq \chi_{c+}, \chi_{c-} \leq P$ and, on the N-dimensional unit volume, $0 \leq$
$\frac{\Pi_j(1-c_j)}{\Pi_j \rho_j}, \frac{\Pi_j c_j}{\Pi_j \rho_j} \leq 1$, so that $0 \leq \mathbb{S}_2 \leq 1$. Then $\Delta_2 = 1 - \mathbb{S}_2$, and ranges from 0
to 1, with increasing values indicating better dispersion throughout the search
space.

It should be noted that for high-dimensionality problems, the Δ_2 component of the dispersion index usually becomes less important. As was described
in Chap. 2, this is because, as dimensionality increases, the probability of finding any population members in any given search-space segment approaches
zero unless the population is very large.

The total search-space population dispersion can then be computed using the intermediate calculations for the $\mathbb{S}$ components:

$$\mathbb{S} = \mathbb{S}_1 + \mathbb{S}_2$$

$$= \max_j \left[\frac{\left[|I_{Uoj} - (I_{cj} + Pc_j^2)| \right]}{P} \right]$$

$$+ \max \left[\frac{\left| \sum_P \chi_{c+} - \text{INT}\left[\left(\frac{\Pi_j (1-c_j)}{\Pi_j \rho_j} \right) P \right] \right|}{P}, \frac{\left| \sum_P \chi_{c-} - \text{INT}\left[\left(\frac{\Pi_j c_j}{\Pi_j \rho_j} \right) P \right] \right|}{P} \right].$$

$$(4.43)$$

The total dispersion index, therefore, with increasing values indicating increasing dispersion, and scaled from 0.0 to 1.0, is computed as:

$$\Delta = \Delta_1 + \Delta_2 = \frac{1.75 - \mathbb{S}}{1.75}. \tag{4.44}$$

While it is still theoretically possible, when using the dispersion index, to mis-classify a distribution as more or less uniform than it actually is using these combined techniques, the distribution would have to be symmetric along multiple search-space diagonals and symmetric around the center of the search space in specific configurations to provide misleading measures of uniformity using the dispersion index. It is considered to be unlikely that this type of deceptive population distribution will be encountered very often in EA practice.

4.2.4 Demonstration and Interpretation of the Dispersion Index

We will illustrate the usefulness of the dispersion index, Δ, through analysis of the 2-dimensional distributions shown in Figs. 4.10 through 4.13 and, lastly, a reasonably uniform 5-dimensional distribution (created using a method to be described in later chapters). The results are shown in Table 4.2.

As can be seen, this diversity measure effectively quantifies the uniformity of the search-space coverage. The "open areas" in deceptive sequences #1 and #2 are larger than those of the random number sequence, and this is reflected

Table 4.2. Dispersion index Δ

Distribution	$\mathbb{S}_1$	$\mathbb{S}_2$	$\mathbb{S}$	Δ
Random	0.268592	0.100000	0.368592	0.789376
2-D Placed Points	0.250325	0.000000	0.250325	0.856597
Deceptive Sequence #1	0.249076	0.240000	0.489076	0.720528
Deceptive Sequence #2	0.250325	0.260000	0.510325	0.708386
5-D Placement	0.250652	0.060000	0.310652	0.822500

in the lower values of Δ for those distributions. The spatial coverage of the 5-dimensional distribution is slightly less uniform than that of the 2-dimensional placed-point distribution. This results in a somewhat smaller value of Δ for the 5-dimensional distribution than for the 2-dimensional distribution.

Finally, this new and more effective search-space diversity measure Δ carries a computational complexity only slightly larger than the basic computation of the sum of the moments of inertia described earlier in this chapter, and is also linear in population size P.

4.3 Summary

The first section of this chapter addressed traditional methods of diversity measurement for EA studies. In this section we introduced two new computationally efficient methods for computing the most commonly used population diversity measures. Using these new methods, the computational complexity of the calculation of population diversity increases linearly with P. These new methods of computing these diversity measures were then extended to non-binary alphabets. For larger alphabets, the size of the alphabet increases the complexity of the moment of inertia calculations, but the increase is linear in alphabet size.

The second section of this chapter addressed the shortcomings of the traditional measures of diversity relative to their measurement of search-space coverage. A new measure of the uniformity of the dispersion of the population throughout a search space, the dispersion index, Δ, was developed and presented. The dispersion index is based on the moments of inertia ideas combined with concepts from discrepancy theory. The mathematical foundations of the dispersion index were presented and an example of its usage was provided.

5

A New EA for Dynamic Problems

5.1 Overview

Chapter 3 identified possible EA enhancements from nature and engineering that could improve the performance of EAs in dynamic environments. Key to these techniques was the management of diversity. Diversity management was identified as a method for ensuring continued exploration of the search space to identify possible changes. Chapter 4 provided the basis for an improved method for measuring the diversity that is more appropriate to dynamic fitness landscapes: the dispersion index. As discussed in Chap. 1, diversity maintenance has undergone initial investigations in the context of dynamic fitness landscapes; however, the quantification of the amount of diversity needed remains largely unexplored. In this chapter we provide the design details for an enhanced EA that permits us to exploit our new understanding of diversity and dispersion, and quantify the need for dispersion in dynamic fitness landscapes. This new EA is very flexible in controlling the amount of population dispersion at any time in an EA run, and addresses the problem of detecting changes in the fitness landscape. These features permit us to conduct experiments to quantitatively identify diversity needs for different types of dynamic problems.

5.2 New EA Design Goals

Recalling that we are trying to enhance an EA's detection of and response to fitness landscape changes, we have identified several design goals for the new algorithm. These goals are related to controlling population diversity, and adaptive information exploitation.

5.2.1 Automatic Detection of and Response to Fitness Landscape Changes

We would like our EA to detect and respond to actual and relevant changes in the fitness landscape. Response mechanisms to fitness landscape changes should only be triggered when they will improve EA performance.

5.2.2 Dispersion Control

Several researchers have confirmed the intuition that diversity maintenance is needed to provide the explorative power for EAs to operate in dynamic fitness landscapes [27], [65], [4], [28]. Having shown that a more appropriate intuition should be "dispersion" rather than "diversity," we would like our new EA to have the ability to introduce and maintain desired levels of dispersion in the population. This dispersion control should be focused on increasing the search-space coverage when that is necessary for exploration and reducing the search-space coverage when search refinement is necessary.

5.2.3 Growth Capability for Adaptive Information Exploitation

As more information is gathered about the performance of EAs with differing population dispersion levels in various environments, we would like our EA architecture to facilitate dynamic changes in population dispersion to any level desired. Additionally, we would like our architecture to facilitate the gathering of information about the fitness landscape change characteristics so that the EA behavior can be modified to accommodate the current landscape dynamics.

5.3 New EA Architecture

In order to accomplish the desired goals above, we need an EA architecture that facilitates the memory of previous fitness evaluations for samples of the search space and the re-sampling of points of the search space to identify changes. The overall concept of the enhanced EA involves the use of *sentinels*, which have the following definition and attributes:

- Sentinels constitute a subset of the population that is uniformly distributed through the search space upon initialization.
- Sentinels are regular members of the population for selection and crossover operations but are stationary and are not, themselves, replaced or mutated.

By using sentinels to continuously sample the same points in the search space, we can allow the EA to continuously run during dynamic landscape changes and continuously produce useful problem solutions that reflect the current landscape dynamics.

Later paragraphs in this chapter will identify the use and justification of the sentinel attributes, as well as provide more specific design details. An overview diagram of the operation of the sentinel-based EA is provided as Fig. 5.1.

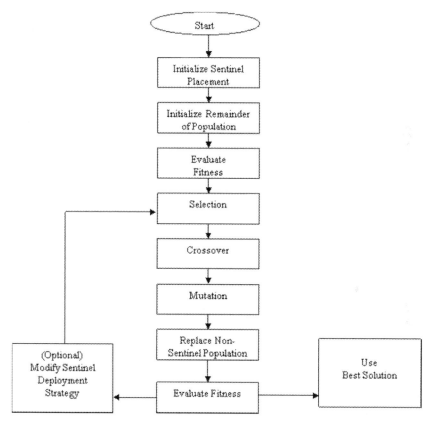

Fig. 5.1. Overview of the sentinel EA operation

5.3.1 Combined Change Detection and Dispersion Maintenance

Through our use of sentinels, we ensure that whatever portion of our population we dedicate to dispersion maintenance will be spread evenly throughout the search space. Whenever a landscape shift occurs, the part of the population that has started to converge near a found peak may suddenly find itself at lower fitness. At this point, sentinels in other parts of the search space will get an increased opportunity to mate and create offspring that are spread throughout the search space, immediately increasing the dispersion of the population. This behavior of the sentinel-based EA is a form of "auto-detection" of fitness landscape changes that is capable of avoiding the pitfalls discussed earlier regarding the detection of landscape changes and the determination that the changes are relevant.

Sentinels also automatically detect and respond to changes in the fitness landscape that would go undetected by other techniques. Sentinels sample regions of the search space continuously and do not abandon them as the algorithm progresses. This continuous search-space surveillance permits response to fitness improvements in regions of the search space that would have been abandoned early in the operation of an ordinary EA. Without this augmented search-space coverage, fitness improvements to previously low fitness areas would go undetected.

5.3.2 Reduction in Maximum Error

The maximum positional error between the global maximum and a member of the population is also reduced through the use of sentinels. Indeed, with sentinels evenly spread through the search space, one can explicitly control the maximum possible distance between a new global maximum position and a population member through selection of the appropriate number of sentinels. For real problems, however, search spaces are generally too large to practically control performance within desired bounds through sentinel placement alone.

5.3.3 Potential for Adaptive Change Response Using Sentinels

Because sentinels sample the same point in the search space repeatedly, a sentinel-based architecture facilitates easy addition of memory to identify whether the landscape change is large or small, trending or not, and how frequently changes occur. Furthermore, by introducing communication among the sentinels, it can be readily determined whether the landscape change is global or local.

With this type of information about the landscape dynamics, it may be possible to adaptively exploit this information to improve our EA response. For example, it may be determined that some types of changes require more or less population dispersion. The new EA architecture is able to dynamically change the number of sentinels, and therefore facilitates addition of this type of adaptive behavior.

Before considering any adaptive additions, however, we first need to examine the effects of the presence of sentinels in various dynamic environments. These effects will be examined in detail in Chap. 8, and further discussion of the potential for adaptive features of the sentinel-based EA will be deferred until Chap. 10, but there are several important design issues that remain to be addressed in the implementation of sentinels in an EA.

5.4 Sentinel Placement

5.4.1 Overview

When considering the introduction of stationary sentinels into an EA population, the question of appropriate sentinel placement in the search space becomes a significant issue. We could just randomly place the sentinels, as Grefenstette does with his random immigrant EA enhancement [28], but since we will be using a relatively small number of sentinels, it would require many EA runs to approximate a uniform sampling of the search space. This defeats our goal of improved performance. We desire a more uniform coverage of the search space with our sentinel placement to more readily detect and respond to any changes in the fitness landscape. Figures 5.2 and 5.3 illustrate the motivation for examining the sentinel placement problem. Figure 5.2 illustrates this problem by showing a 2-dimensional search space with 50 points which were plotted by using a random number generator independently for each dimension. Figure 5.3 is the same 2-dimensional search space with 50 points plotted by the heuristic sentinel placement algorithm developed in this chapter. The significant improvement in search-space coverage, and attendant improved ability to respond to changes throughout the search space, are obvious.

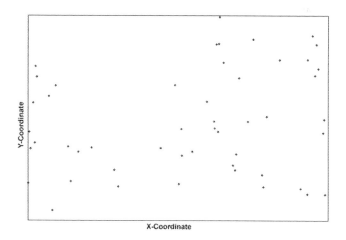

Fig. 5.2. Fifty randomly plotted points

How do we maximize the effectiveness of sentinel landscape exploration with each sentinel? Another way of expressing the question is, "If there is one more sentinel to place in n-dimensional space, where is the most effective place

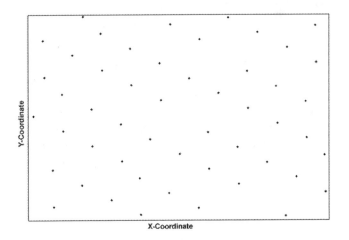

Fig. 5.3. Fifty points plotted by a sentinel placement algorithm

to put it to maximize search space coverage?" Much research in partitioning high-dimensional spaces has been dedicated to partitioning existing data sets into groups using global and local distance measures for information search and retrieval. Here we have the opposite problem. We want to place a small number of data points evenly throughout a multi-dimensional space. For this, we must borrow concepts from current research in computational geometry and sequence generation and adapt them to our purposes. In this section we will describe our method for sentinel placement.

It should be noted that the issue of uniform sentinel placement is the same as the often ignored issue among EA researchers regarding population initialization. Ensuring uniform search-space coverage during population initialization would potentially reduce the need for as many EA runs as are currently required to achieve good EA performance. This issue has occasionally been recognized [32], [11], but little work has been done to adequately address the problem. The sentinel placement algorithm developed in the following paragraphs may be equally useful for population initialization for EAs in general, and this idea will receive an initial examination in Chap. 9.

5.4.2 Desired Features of a Sentinel Placement Algorithm

There are several desired features of any sentinel placement algorithm. They are:

- Extreme computational efficiency. The use of sentinels is part of an approach to improve the efficiency of EAs in dynamic fitness landscapes, so computationally intensive methods for placing them, or evaluating their placement, that need to occur during the EA operation defeat this purpose. If any analysis is required for placing sentinels for a new problem environment, that analysis must be able to be performed off line.

- Reasonably uniform search-space coverage. Although optimal coverage might be desired, current research in computational geometry involves very computationally intensive techniques to approach this goal [26]. The first of the desired features forces us to settle for reasonably uniform coverage.
- Scalable to any number of dimensions for problems of arbitrary complexity.

5.4.3 The Placement Problem

Let us first address this problem in symmetric search space. We are using sentinels to detect changes to features in the search space, so we are trying to spread the sentinels evenly through the search space to maximize search-space coverage. Let us take a deeper look at more precisely what this means.

We desire to improve the search capability of the sentinels by separating them in the search space such that their positioning maximizes the probability of detection of a landscape feature change. As discussed in Sect. 2.4.1, in the general case, for any specific number of sentinels, this is equivalent to solving an N-dimensional sphere packing problem. In this case, however, the problem is expressed in terms of the packing space size and the number of spheres, and must be solved for the sphere radius and the coordinates of the packed spheres. The sphere radius would then be the detection range of the landscape feature change ε, and the sphere center coordinates would be the sentinel position. While much research has been done in sphere packing problems [59], [56], efficient methods for solving the above problem have not been identified. Remembering that we are trying to improve the computational efficiency and effectiveness of EAs in dynamic fitness landscapes, adding computationally intense processes to the problem solution is counterproductive to that goal.

The problem becomes more difficult when using a variable number of sentinels. We would like the ability to add sentinels to cover the unoccupied search-space volume without moving previously placed sentinels. This is necessary to allow for uninterrupted identification of changes and trends in the landscape.

The identification of the largest unoccupied volume for the placement of the "next" sentinel in N-space already occupied by a population of sentinels is an interesting problem in itself. The common N-dimensional space partitioning techniques such as Voronoi diagrams and Delaunay triangulation [68] do not assist in the identification of the largest unoccupied N-dimensional volume. All of these methods can result in an unintentional division of the largest unoccupied volume by inappropriate space partitioning edge placement, rather than point placement.

Another area of research that could be used for placing points in N-dimensional space includes research into meshing techniques such as t-m-s nets [49]. As a powerful mechanism for placing points uniformly in N-dimensional space, t-m-s nets cover space in base b in dimension N, requiring b^N points to assure uniform spatial coverage. However, because the process starts by partitioning the space into b^N cells and we wish to use a varying number of points without re-positioning previous points, the mesh-generating techniques are generally inappropriate for our application.

Since we are trying to place all sentinels such that the distance to a potential landscape change is minimized, ideally we would like to place an additional sentinel into an existing field of sentinels at the midpoint of the largest unoccupied symmetrical volume. What we are in need of is a computationally efficient heuristic algorithm that is better than a simple random number generator in efficiently placing sentinels uniformly throughout a search space, occupying unoccupied volumes first. The specialty field in mathematics that has done some exploration into this type of problem is called low-discrepancy sequence generation [19]. The key idea in this field of mathematics is discrepancy measurement. Discrepancy measurement identifies how uniformly a set of points samples a search space, and was described in Chap. 4.

Much of the research into low-discrepancy sequences is involved in establishing upper and lower bounds on the discrepancy of various sequences, through algorithmic proofs or example construction. The research in this field is usually focused on finding sequences with the smallest values of discrepancy in the limit [13], [1]. There is, however, usually no evidence that these sequences will perform well in an application such as ours, where only a small number of points near the beginning of the sequence will actually be used. Additionally, our application has severe computational efficiency requirements, and none of the research appears to adequately address this requirement. Therefore, the discussion of discrepancy theory in Chap. 4, while providing useful concepts for diversity measurement, is not useful for placing sentinels. Because of this, we have derived our own methodology for efficiently placing sentinels into a search space of arbitrary dimension. Using the current research in sequence generation, we have derived a heuristic set of rules for an N-dimensional space point sequence generator that has the attributes we desire for our application.

5.4.4 Heuristic Sentinel Placement

For the construction of our sentinel placement algorithm, we used some of the research on the $k\alpha$ sequence for an irrational α. This is a well-studied sequence and is known to be uniformly distributed modulo 1 [19].

This sequence has been extended into N dimensions, through what is known as the Kroenecker sequence [1]. The Kroenecker sequence is based on the following theorem, quoted from [19]. Let $\beta_1, \ldots, \beta_N \in \Re$. Then:

Theorem 5.1. *The N-dimensional sequence $x_k = (k\beta_1, \ldots, k\beta_N)$ is uniformly distributed modulo 1 if and only if $1, \beta_1, \ldots, \beta_N$ are linearly independent over the integers $\mathcal{Z}$.*

This is an extension of the $k\alpha$ sequence since, for $\beta_1 \ldots \beta_N$ to be linearly independent over the integers, there are no integers $m_i \in \mathcal{Z}$ such that $1, m_1\beta_1 + \ldots + m_N\beta_N = 0$. In other words, the βs must be irrational. So, by our notation convention, we will refer to these numbers in future references as αs (i.e., $k\alpha_1, \ldots, k\alpha_N$).

Despite mathematical study of the Kroenecker sequence since the 1950s, as an interesting sequence that is known to be uniformly distributed modulo 1, it is only in the mid-1990s that new bounds were shown on this sequence's discrepancy. While the proofs are unwieldy, it has been shown that for a sequence of P points, kx_i, where x_i consists of badly approximable irrational numbers $(\alpha_1 \ldots \alpha_N)$, the discrepancy is [19]:

$$\mathbb{D}_P = \mathcal{O}(P^{\frac{-1}{N}}(logP)^2). \tag{5.1}$$

Although mathematicians do not believe this to be the best possible discrepancy for this sequence, a discrepancy limit of this size does not place this sequence among the sequences that most rapidly converge to uniform for large P [19].

However, as mentioned earlier, we are not really interested in theoretical convergence for large sequences. We are interested in the uniformity of the distribution of the first few points (perhaps as high as several hundred or a thousand) of the sequence. The extreme computational efficiency of this algorithm, once the αs are identified, makes it very attractive for our application.

So our contribution here is to devise a set of rules for using the concepts of the Kroenecker sequence to construct a reasonably uniformly distributed set of points in N-space for the range of dimensions and range of number of points of interest for EA applications. We will then use those rules to derive a set of αs that EA practitioners and researchers can use. To understand the problem, we will first demonstrate the types of initial non-uniformity that the Kroenecker sequence can generate. Figures 5.4 and 5.5 illustrate two of the types of non-uniform initial point distributions that can be generated by badly chosen, but irrational, αs. Each of these sequences will be uniformly distributed in the long run, but they are very bad choices with respect to the initial few points.

What we need is "good interdimensional mixing" for the first few hundred points of the sequence. To accomplish this, we have developed a few heuristic rules. The rules will first be delineated, then the reasons for each of these heuristics will be described.

1. Base the incremental intervals for each dimension on multiples of the "Golden Ratio" which is: $\phi = \frac{\sqrt{5}+1}{2}$.
2. Select the multiples of ϕ for each dimension from sequences of prime numbers.
3. Examine the resultant modulo 1 sequences for the quasi-period with which they revisit a value near the initial value (this is done by examining the sequential distance difference as described below). If a multiplier results in

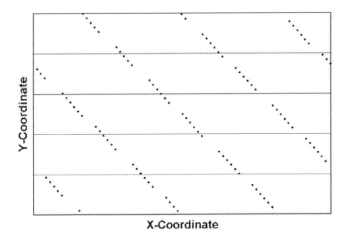

Fig. 5.4. Fifty Kroenecker sequence points #1

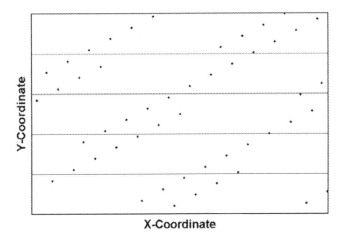

Fig. 5.5. Fifty Kroenecker sequence points #2

either a very short or trivial sequence of sequential differences, or closely matches the sequential difference sequence of a previously selected multiplier, do not use that multiplier; use the next prime number multiplier instead.

The reasons for these heuristics are fairly straightforward. First, to achieve good mixing in the initial points of the sequence, we need a "very" irrational number. Irrational numbers are classified by how easy they are to approximate with continued-fraction ratios of integers. For example, $\sqrt{2}$, which is irrational, would be inappropriate to use since it is well approximated by the continued-fraction sequence:

$$\sqrt{2} = 1 + \cfrac{1}{2 + \cfrac{1}{2 + \cfrac{1}{2 + \frac{1}{2+\text{etc.}}}}}. \tag{5.2}$$

The "Golden Ratio" mentioned previously, normally represented by ϕ, is the irrational number that is most poorly approximated through continued fractions [2]. This is the obvious choice for uniformly distributed placement, since the more irrational α is, the more uniformly distributed is the first part of the sequence of P points $P_i = \{K_i\alpha\}$, where $K_i = 1, 2, 3, \ldots, P$ [1]. However, the use of ϕ only guarantees best placement in one dimension. If the same α (or any integer multiple of the same α) is used for a Kroenecker sequence in more than one dimension, the points are merely placed along a diagonal in those dimensions. This is why the Kroenecker sequence requires linear independence among $\mathcal{Z}$. Furthermore, since it can be very difficult to prove that a number is either irrational or linearly independent over $\mathcal{Z}$, we will again return to the fact that we are only interested in the placement behavior of the first few points in an infinite sequence. This brings us to the second heuristic rule.

The second rule is to select the multiples of ϕ for each dimension from sequences of prime numbers, avoiding the prime numbers 1 and 2. What we need to accomplish here is to force the pair-wise relationship between dimensions to be irrational. Ratios of prime numbers approximate irrational numbers and this method makes the ratios of the step sizes between any two dimensions relatively irrational.[1] This approximation is adequate for our purposes, as long as the sequences generated provide good placement and good interdimensional mixing. Since, however, multiples of ϕ do not necessarily have the same placement uniformity as ϕ, we come to the third heuristic rule.

This third heuristic rule is designed to improve mixing across multiple dimensions. In a sequence $kZ_i\alpha$ modulo 1, for $k = 1, 2, 3, \ldots$ and $Z_i \in \mathcal{Z}$, values within a distance of ε of the first point are visited quasi-periodically, with the sequential differences between these quasi-periods forming an easily recognizable pattern, but with occasional and irregular breaks in the pattern. An example of this is shown as Fig. 5.6. In this figure, the distance to the starting point of a Kroenecker sequence is plotted for 50 points. As can be seen, for $\varepsilon = 0.10$ the distance is less than ε at $k = 6, 14, 18, 22, 26, 31, 35, 39, 43, 48\ldots$. The sequential difference between the k values are $8, 4, 4, 4, 5, 4, 4, 4, 4, \ldots$. When these sequential differences form trivial patterns like this (or, for example, $1, 1, 1, 1, 1, 1, 5, 1, 1, 1, 1, 1, 1, 5$), or are identical to the patterns already

---

[1] Sequential very large prime numbers must also not be used, since the ratio of two sequential very large prime numbers closely approximates 1.0 and will result in a violation of the next heuristic rule.

selected for other prime multipliers, the fill pattern across multiple dimensions is usually not adequately mixed. These sequences are easily checked using a simple spreadsheet, and, if an undesired sequence is encountered, the next prime number in the sequence should be selected as the multiplier.

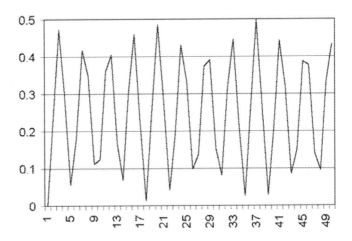

Fig. 5.6. Quasi-Periodic Distance to the First Point

The resultant heuristic sentinel placement algorithm works as follows. First, scale and offset all search-space dimensions as necessary to set each dimensional range from 0 to 1. Second, randomly place the initial sentinel point, x_i, within the search space, for i equal 1 to N. Finally, compute the coordinates of each subsequent point P, $x_{i,p} \in P$, as:

$$x_{i,p} = \text{mod}1[x_{i,p-1} + Z_i\phi], \tag{5.3}$$

where the Z_is are selected for each dimension in accordance with the heuristic rules specified.

As can be seen, the coordinates of each point can easily (and very computationally efficiently) be determined from the location of the previous point, once the Z_is are selected through an off-line process for the range of dimensions and sentinel population sizes appropriate for the problem domain. Note that nothing more need be known about the problem space than the number of dimensions and the approximate size of the population of sentinels to be used, and that this information is used off-line in a simple spreadsheet calculation.

In later sections of this chapter, we complete the spreadsheet analysis and apply the heuristic rules to provide a recommended set of prime numbers for use as Z_i in (5.3) for up to 12-dimensional problems.

5.4.5 Placement Quality

Figures 5.7, 5.8, 5.9, and 5.10 show examples of 2-dimensional projections, of a 5-dimensional placement of sentinels using this algorithm with prime-number multipliers of 41, 43, 47, 59, and 83 (omitting several primes in accordance with the heuristic rules). The starting point of 41 was chosen arbitrarily. It should be remembered, however, that the appearance of uniformity in lower-dimensionality projections of a higher-dimensional search space does not guarantee uniformity of the spatial coverage in the higher dimension, so an analysis of the uniformity of the distribution in the search space for the selected parameters must be conducted. The dispersion index, Δ, using these prime multipliers is provided later in this chapter.

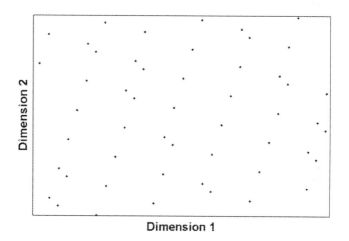

Fig. 5.7. Dimensions 1 and 2 of a 5-dimensional sequence of 50 points

5.4.6 Sentinel Placement Algorithm in High-Dimension Search Spaces

High-dimension search spaces require a large set of prime numbers that obey the heuristic rules for selection. These can be difficult to find, although all effort expended in finding them is performed off-line and does not affect the EA performance. More important, however, is the fact that it is probably not worth the effort. In Chap. 2, when we were discussing the problems associated with change detection, we noted how rapidly the distances between points increase with search-space dimensionality. With very large distances

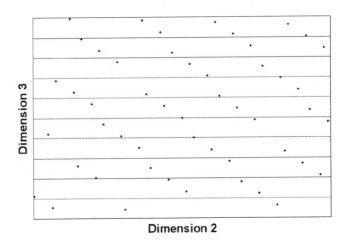

Fig. 5.8. Dimensions 2 and 3 of a 5-dimensional sequence of 50 points

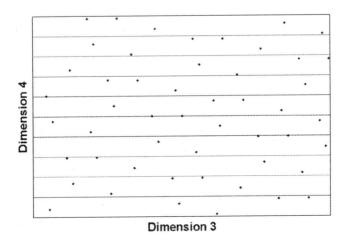

Fig. 5.9. Dimensions 3 and 4 of a 5-dimensional sequence of 50 points

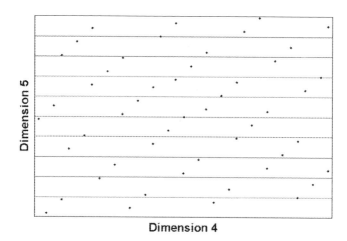

Fig. 5.10. Dimensions 4 and 5 of a 5-dimensional sequence of 50 points

between only a few points, the benefit of placing population members "uniformly" versus "randomly" diminishes. For this and other reasons, several mathematicians have expressed doubts about the usefulness of uniform distribution methods for dimensions higher than about 12 [52], [13]. Because of this, if the dimensionality of the problem is greater than 12, random sentinel placement is recommended. Other sentinel-based EA benefits, such as landscape-change identification, trend recognition, and EA adaptation based on the type of fitness landscape change detected, are anticipated to be useful in higher dimensions, so it is only the placement algorithm that needs to be modified for high-dimensional search spaces. This issue will be examined further in the experiments of Chaps. 8 and 9.

5.4.7 Recommended Prime Multiplier Values for Dimensions 1 Through 12

Table 5.1 provides recommended α values for 1 through 12 dimensions that were derived using the heuristic rules described in this chapter. The table also provides the dispersion index, Δ, along with the intermediate calculations, $\mathbb{S}_1$, $\mathbb{S}_2$, and $\mathbb{S}$ for populations of the first 50 points generated using these αs. (Recall that the dispersion index, Δ, measures the uniformity of the population dispersion and has a maximum value of 1.00 for a completely uniform distribution.) While these are not guaranteed to be the optimal αs for use with any specific EA problem, these prime numbers are known to provide acceptably uniform distributions for the first 200 points in dimensions up through 12.

Table 5.1. Prime αs and dispersion indices for 50 points, dimensions 1 through 12

Dimension	α	$\mathbb{S}_1$	$\mathbb{S}_2$	$\mathbb{S}$	Δ
1	41	0.0025	0.0200	0.0225	0.9871
2	43	0.0077	0.0200	0.0277	0.9841
3	47	0.0121	0.0400	0.0521	0.9702
4	59	0.0121	0.0100	0.0221	0.9874
5	83	0.0158	0.0300	0.0458	0.9738
6	107	0.0158	0.0200	0.0358	0.9795
7	109	0.0158	0.0100	0.0258	0.9853
8	173	0.0158	0.0100	0.0258	0.9853
9	311	0.0158	0.0100	0.0258	0.9853
10	373	0.0158	0.0000	0.0158	0.9910
11	401	0.0158	0.0000	0.0000	0.9999
12	409	0.0158	0.0000	0.0158	0.9910

5.4.8 Sentinel Placement in Asymmetric Search Spaces

Up until this point, we have only been describing sentinel placement in symmetric search spaces. Fortunately, the transition to asymmetric spaces is quite straightforward. This is a trivial process since sentinel placement is so computationally efficient. Simply compute the sentinel positions as if the search space was symmetric in all axes, then disregard any points falling outside the search space. Compute additional points, continuing to discard those falling outside of the search space, until the desired number fall within the search space.

5.5 Summary

In this chapter we have presented the basic information about our new sentinel-based EA architecture for dynamic fitness landscapes. Specifically, we have identified the features to be incorporated into the architecture and the justification for each. Additionally, we have provided an algorithm and heuristic rules to solve the complicated problem of uniform placement of an arbitrary number of sentinels in a search space of arbitrary dimensionality. We have applied this algorithm and the heuristic rules to compute a set of prime numbers for use with the sentinel placement algorithm. We have also mentioned that the sentinel placement algorithm derived herein might be useful in ensuring better search-space coverage during population initialization for static EAs. This will be addressed in Chap. 9, but first we must describe the experimental methods and provide additional implementation details regarding the basic EA that will be used throughout the remainder of this book.

6

Experimental Methods

6.1 Overview

In this chapter we will provide the details of the experimental methodology used in this research. The second section of this chapter will provide background regarding dynamic fitness landscape test problem generators. The third section will identify the requirements for a test problem generator in dynamic environments. The fourth section will provide the details of a test problem generator that was developed as part of this research to address the issues identified in the second section and the requirements identified in the third section. The fifth section will describe the details of the test problems examined in this study. The next section will describe experiments used to compare the results of our new technique to previous EA techniques used for dynamic environments. Finally, the last section of this chapter will describe the specific experiments conducted to examine the usefulness of our sentinel placement algorithm for population initialization in EAs working in static environments.

6.2 Problem Generator Background

Historically, studies of EAs in dynamic environments have used only a few, limited fitness functions. Recently, researchers have developed custom dynamic test functions to examine specific EA performance issues [67] and suggestions for a reusable dynamic test problem generator have been made in [45], and [12], and a standard dynamic knapsack problem has been suggested in [23]. As has been shown in the study of EAs in static environments, comparative studies of the effectiveness of various EAs in dynamic environments will require rigorous and standardized test functions. These functions should have a simple representation mechanism, but still present a wide range of complexity and sophisticated dynamics that can be reproduced and unambiguously described in an elementary manner. Further, the dynamic behavior of the test problems should include movement of any global optima throughout the entire range of the search space. In this chapter, we describe a dynamic test function generator, with these characteristics, that we have developed to facilitate further understanding of the effectiveness of different EA implementations in different types of dynamic environments.

6.3 Generator Requirements

In the building of a test problem generator for dynamic landscapes, an important consideration is the range of dynamic behavior that the generator should be able to produce. In the simplest non-stationary problems, the overall shape (morphology) of the fitness landscape is constant, but it drifts along one or more axes over time. It is relatively easy, for example, to take any 2-dimensional static landscape $f(x, y)$ and make it vary over time in this simple sense by redefining it as $g(x, y, t) = f(x_{t-1} + \delta x_t, y_{t-1} + \delta y_t)$, and by providing the "motion algorithm" for computing δx_t and δy_t. The motion itself can have several properties including its speed (rapid/slow relative to EA time), periodic/aperiodic, etc. The focus here is typically on how well an EA can follow (track) a moving landscape.

More difficult and more interesting are landscapes whose morphology changes over time (see, for example, [25] or [28]). Providing a simple way to construct interesting test problems of this type is the goal of the work presented here. We do so by focusing on the "peaks" in a landscape and consider how peaks might independently change over time.

6.3.1 Changing Fitness Peak Heights

There are many real-world problems that can be modeled by simply allowing the heights of fitness peaks to change over time reflecting, for example, changes in the cost of raw materials, changes in consumer preferences, etc., resulting in global optima becoming local optima and vice versa. Traditional EAs have no difficulty converging on initially high fitness peaks, but the loss of diversity in the population makes it difficult for them to adapt to this type of change.

6.3.2 Changing Fitness Peak Shapes

Closely related to changes in peak heights are changes in their shape (e.g., tall and narrow, short and wide, etc.). Alone, shape changes often do not affect the performance of traditional EAs much. However, in conjunction with other simultaneous changes, they can pose considerable difficulty by making the global optimum more difficult to detect.

6.3.3 Changing Fitness Peak Locations

Another source of difficulty for current EAs is fitness peaks that change location [25]. EAs with populations lacking in diversity have difficulty tracking such changes. Tracking becomes even more difficult if the peaks can move independently of one another.

6.3.4 The Dynamics of Change

So far we have focused on *what* has been changing over time. Equally important is *how* things are changing, that is, the dynamics of change. The two most common dynamics studied are a slowly drifting motion (e.g., [3] or [4]) and an oscillatory motion (e.g., [17] or [42]).

Clearly, the form of the dynamics will play an important role in the kind of modifications one might make to existing EAs. To handle slowly drifting changes it may be sufficient to incrementally increase population diversity through adaptive local-search operators [65]. However, oscillating changes are likely to require more fundamental changes such as diploid representations (e.g., [25], [17], or [57]), or additional "memory" functions (e.g., [50] or [42]).

One additional dynamic of interest is that of an abrupt, unexpected, catastrophic change to the fitness landscape, capturing the kinds of effects that power failures have on complex networks, that 10-car accidents have on traffic flow, etc. Triggered mutation operators are one example of the changes made to EAs to handle such dynamics [15].

6.3.5 Problem Generator Requirements Summary

Our stated goal is to develop a test problem generator for dynamic fitness landscapes that provides for easy and systematic testing and evaluation of EAs over a wide range of dynamics as discussed in the previous section. To achieve this a dynamic problem generator should have:

1. Easily modifiable landscape complexity that is scalable to complexity levels representative of problems found in nature.
2. Simple parametric methods to specify the morphological characteristics and changes, including peak re-ordering, peak relocation, and peak re-shaping.
3. Simple methods to specify the type of dynamics to apply including: small steps, large steps, multiple step sizes, recurrent motion, and chaotic motion.
4. Simple representation mechanisms, so that a complex environment with sophisticated dynamics can be unambiguously defined in an elementary manner.
5. Reasonable computational efficiency.

6.4 Problem Generator Description and Features

In this section we describe in detail the features of DF1, our dynamic environment problem generator. In designing DF1 we have adopted the view that the process of specifying a test problem is a two-step process. The first step involves specifying a baseline static landscape of the desired morphological complexity. Having done this, the second step is to add the desired dynamics. We discuss each of these steps in more detail in the following sections.

6.4.1 Specifying the Morphology

To provide a parameterized way of specifying the basic morphology of the landscape, in DF1 we use a "field of cones" of different heights and different slopes randomly scattered across the landscape. This static function is similar to the plane of Gaussian distributions used in [28]. The static function used in DF1 can be specified for any number of dimensions. For visualization purposes we will use 2-dimensional examples or 2-dimensional projections of higher-dimensional examples throughout the remainder of this chapter. In the 2-dimensional case we have:

$$f(X,Y) = max_{i=1,N} \left[H_i - R_i * \sqrt{(X - X_i)^2 + (Y - Y_i)^2} \right]$$

where: N specifies the number of cones in the environment, and each cone is independently specified by its location (X_i, Y_i), its height H_i, and its slope R_i. Each of these independently specified cones are "blended" together using the max function.

Each time the generator is called it produces a randomly generated morphology of this type in which random values for each cone are assigned based on user-specified ranges:

$$H_i \in [Hbase, Hbase + Hrange]$$

$$R_i \in [Rbase, Rbase + Rrange]$$

and

$$X_i \in [-1, 1]$$

$$Y_i \in [-1, 1].$$

There are several advantages to the use of this function as the static basis for the dynamic environment. They include:

1. The ability to represent a wide range of complex landscapes.
2. The surface contains non-differentiable regions.
3. Landscape characteristics are parametrically identified.
4. Fitness values can be easily restricted to be positive (or any other minimum value), if desired.

5. The function is easily extensible to higher-dimensional spaces.
6. The function offers three different features that can be made dynamic (height, location, and slope).

To generate a wide range of static problems of varying complexity, one need only specify the parameters: N (the number of peaks), $Rbase$ (the minimum value of the slope control variable), $Rrange$ (the allowed range for the slope control), $Hbase$ (the minimum cone height), and $Hrange$ (the range of allowed cone heights). Two examples of the variety of fitness landscapes generated by varying these five parameters are illustrated in Figs. 6.1 and 6.2.

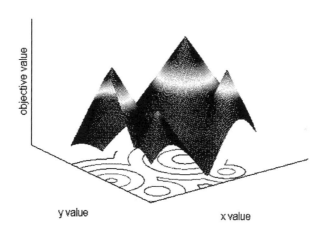

Fig. 6.1. DF1 with $N = 5$, $Hbase = 3$, $Hrange = 3$, $Rbase = 2$, $Rrange = 5$

In Fig. 6.1 we see one of the randomly generated landscapes specified to have 5 peaks of heights ranging from 3 to 6, with slopes ranging from 2 to 7. In Fig. 6.2 we see a much more complex randomly generated landscape specified to have 500 peaks of heights ranging from 50 to 75, and slopes ranging from 100 to 120.

6.4.2 Specifying the Dynamics

As discussed earlier, it is desirable to provide a simple mechanism for describing a wide range of dynamic performance. Since we change the dynamic features of the environment by discrete step sizes, we would like a simple method

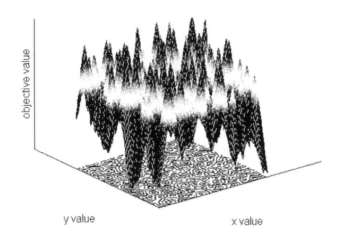

Fig. 6.2. DF1 with $N = 500$, $Hbase = 50$, $Hrange = 25$, $Rbase = 100$, $Rrange = 20$

for controlling the generation of a variety of different step sizes. One method for generating a variety of dynamics with the change of a single parameter is to use a 1-dimensional, non-linear function that has simple bifurcation transitions to progressively more complex behavior. One of the most common and well-studied functions with this behavior is the logistics function given by:

$$Y_i = A * Y_{(i-1)} * (1 - Y_{(i-1)})$$

where: A is a constant, and Y_i is the value at iteration i.

A bifurcation map of the logistics function is provided in Fig. 6.3. This figure shows the values of Y that can be generated on each iteration of the logistics function for values of A between 1 and 4. For example, if a value of 2.2 is chosen, the logistics function will generate a constant Y value of 0.5455 on each iteration. For a larger A of 2.9, a larger constant Y value of 0.6552 is generated.

As A is increased, more complicated dynamic behavior emerges. Values slightly larger than the first bifurcation point generate two different values of Y for alternate iterations. For example, values of 3.3 and 3.4 generate pairs of Y values {0.8236, 0.4794} and {0.8420, 0.4520} respectively. As larger A values are chosen the function bifurcates again and provides more complex behavior. At $A = 3.5$, the Y values generated are {0.3828, 0.5009, 0.8269, 0.8750}. Still larger values of A generate chaotic sequences of Y values within the range shown in Fig. 6.3.

In DF1 we use the Y values produced on each iteration to select our step sizes for the dynamic portions of our environment. More specifically, we attach

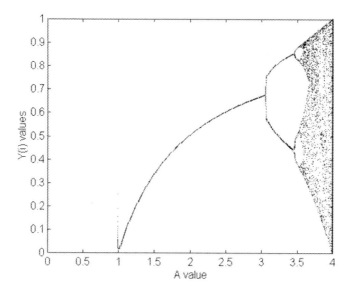

Fig. 6.3. The logistics function

a logistics function with a specified A value to each dynamic entity. The result is a simple procedure for users to obtain complex dynamics by specifying:

1. The number of peaks in the landscape that will move.
2. Whether the motion will be applied to the height of the peaks, the slope of the peaks, the x location of the peaks, the y location of the peaks, or any combination thereof.

The particular value of A chosen for each of the moving features specifies whether the movement will be small same-sized steps, large same-sized steps, steps of few different sizes, or chaotically changing step sizes. As suggested by Fig. 6.3, we require that the values chosen for A must be greater than one and less than four.

What remains then is to map the range of Y values produced into appropriately scaled step sizes for the particular dynamic feature. This is accomplished by scaling the Y values to keep the step sizes less than 0.5 (50%) of the user-specified range of values, and then using the step size as a percentage of the range to add to or subtract from the current parameter value. For example, for an individual cone that is increasing dynamically in height, first the current height is computed as a percentage of maximum height:

$$Hpct = H/(Hbase + Hrange).$$

The current Y value is then scaled by a user-supplied height scaling factor and added to the $Hpct$:

$$Hpct = Hpct + Y * Hscale.$$

If this is less than the 100% of the valid range, then the new height value is computed from the percentage value. If it is greater than 100%, then the new value is computed as $Hbase + (100\% - (Hpct - 100\%)) * Hrange$ and the step change sign is reversed. This causes the movement to "bounce" off of the limits of the search space. The sign remains reversed for each iteration until the minimum value of the range is reached, at which point it is reversed again.

Hence, the dynamics of the landscape can be simply and precisely specified by providing:

- $Nummove$ – the number of peaks in motion,
- Ah – the A value for peak height dynamics, if height dynamics are chosen,
- Ar – the A value for cone slope dynamics, if slope dynamics are chosen,
- Ax_i – the A value for i-axis movement dynamics, if movement in x_i is chosen,

and a scaling factor for each A value specified.

6.4.3 Examples

In this section we illustrate a small set of the different types of dynamics that are possible and easily described with this test function. It is possible to generate dynamic functions similar to many of those already studied in the EA literature using this generator. For ease of illustration here, all examples use relatively small, uniform incremental steps (small A values). It is possible, but harder, to visualize dynamics involving larger step sizes, several different fixed step sizes, or chaotic step size selection. The landscape changes can also be made recurrent (similar to the recurrent knapsack problem commonly studied in the EA literature) through selection of the initial configuration and the step size parameter A.

6.4.4 Linear Motion

With DF1 even simple linear motion produces rather interesting dynamics. Consider a simple landscape consisting of several peaks two of which are moving using simple linear motion. As they move, they can hide/expose other peaks as a result of max blending. When they reach user-specified boundaries, they "rebound" like a billiard ball. It is difficult to visualize this without providing a complete movie of the dynamics produced. Figure 6.4 attempts to do so by showing frames 2, 4, and 6 of a movie of two cones (from a larger group of cones) moving in opposite directions in the x–y plane.

If you look carefully, you should see them start out close together in the middle of the landscape, and then move in opposite directions, one to the left and one to the right. As they move, a previously hidden peak in the center emerges.

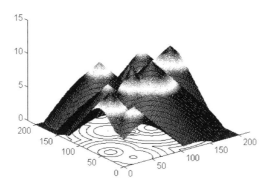

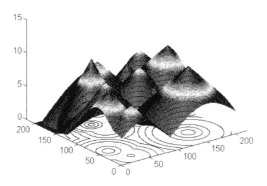

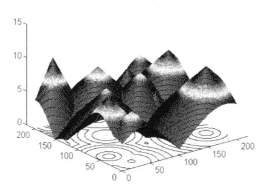

Fig. 6.4. x–y movement of 2 cones, $Ax = Ay = 2.0$, $Xstepscale = 0.15$, $Ystepscale = 0.25$

6.4.5 Changing Cone Shapes

Figure 6.5 shows the changes in the landscape caused by the slope of one cone starting out quite small (resulting in a broad peak that overshadows may others) and increases over time. As the cone's extent narrows, other hidden peaks become visible.

This illustrates a nice property of the generator, namely that even though a fixed number of cones are initially specified, the dynamic complexity of the landscape can change rather dramatically via the masking effect due to the use of *max* blending.

6.4.6 Changing Peak Heights

As a final example, Fig. 6.6 illustrates an environment where the peaks are stationary, but their relative height changes over time.

6.4.7 DF1 Summary

The DF1 test problem generator provides easy methods to reliably reproduce a wide variety of interesting dynamic test problems for use in EA research. Although we have kept things deliberately simple for visualization purposes, the DF1 generator is applicable for use in higher dimensions and can generate a wide variety of increasingly complex dynamics through application of more than one of the available types of dynamics simultaneously and increasing the chosen values of A to provide variable step sizes. C source code for the DF1 problem generator is available for download at:
http://www.rEvolutionaryEngineering.com/download.html.

6.5 Test Problem Description

6.5.1 Test Problem Overview

The test problem generator described in the previous section is capable of generating a very wide range of dynamic performance. For the evaluation of the performance of the sentinel-based EA, several problem types were selected to represent a variety of problem characteristics and complexities. These extend from a fairly simple, 2-dimensional, low-complexity, multi-modal landscape, where most of the landscape is static, but the global optimum moves throughout the landscape; to a complex, 10-dimensional, multi-modal landscape where all of the landscape peaks move chaotically throughout the landscape. Each of these basic types of landscapes is examined for a variety of periods between landscape changes, from static over many generations to changing every few generations.

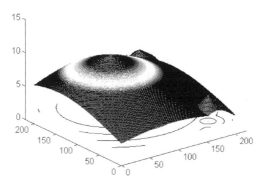

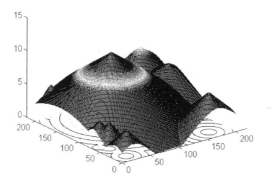

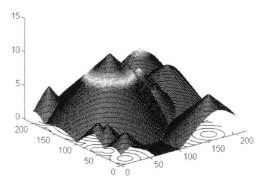

Fig. 6.5. One cone changing slope, $Ar = 2.2$, $Rstepscale = 0.3$

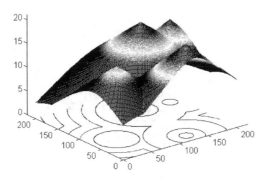

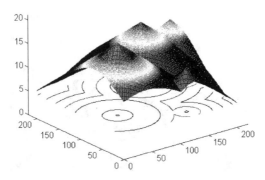

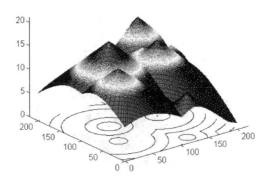

Fig. 6.6. Fourteen cones changing height, $Ah = 1.2$, $Hstepscale = 0.35$

6.5.2 Static Landscape Structures

Four basic static landscape morphologies are studied for the dynamic problems. They are:

- A 2-dimensional, 5-cone configuration, with four cones of the same height and one cone as the global maximum.
- A 2-dimensional, 14-cone configuration, with the heights of 13 of the cones initialized randomly and one cone set to a global maximum.
- A 5-dimensional, 5-cone configuration, with four cones of the same height and one cone set to a global maximum.
- A 10-dimensional, 14-cone configuration, with the heights of 13 of the cones initialized randomly and one cone set to the global maximum.

Examples of 2-dimensional projections of these 5-cone and 14-cone configurations are shown in Figs. 6.7 and 6.8 respectively.

Fig. 6.7. Fitness values of a 2-D projection of 5 cones.

6.5.3 Dynamic Behavior Applied

The dynamic behaviors applied were selected to examine a range of problems from fairly simple to quite complex. To ensure that there is exactly one global

Fig. 6.8. Fitness values of a 2-D projection of 14 cones

optimal peak for each problem, the "overwrite" feature of the DF1 problem generator was used. In every configuration exactly one landscape peak was overwritten with a peak value higher than the maximum range of the other peaks. This global maximum is assigned custom $Hmax$ and $Rmax$ values to describe its characteristics. All position and fitness errors were then measured from this peak.

For the 2-dimensional problems, the 5-cone problem has only the highest cone moving in small steps through the search space, and the 14-cone problem has all cones moving chaotically throughout the search space. In higher dimensions two 5-dimensional versions of the 5-cone problem are implemented: one with all cones independently moving in small steps through the search space, and another where the cone steps are larger. For each of the problems described thus far, the EA performance is examined when the landscape is moved every 10, 20, 30, 40, 50, 60, and 70 generations. The most complex problem tested, the 14-cone configuration with all cones moving chaotically, is implemented in 10 dimensions. This final problem is sufficiently complex that the EA makes little progress with rapid landscape dynamics, so the landscape movements are tested at 30, 60, and 90 generations. As above, the performance data is collected for a number of generations equal to 20 times the movement period (i.e., if the movement period is 10 generations, the EA is run for 200 generations, if the movement period is 50 generations, the EA is run for 1000 generations, and if the movement period is 90 generations, the EA is run for 1800 generations).

For convenience, individual problems will be referred to by a tuple of the identifying problem characteristics, with number of cones as the first number, followed by the number of dimensions, N, the number of cones moving, M, and the type of movement as small, S, large, L, or chaotic, C. The 14-cone problem in 10 dimensions with all cones moving chaotically, for example, will be referred to as 14N10M14C. Table 6.1 provides the DF1 parameters used to create the dynamic fitness landscapes for these problems.

Table 6.1. DF1 parameters for dynamic problem configurations

Param.	5N2M1S	14N2M14C	5N5M5S	5N5M5L	14N10M14C
Hbase	60.0	1.0	60.0	60.0	1.0
Hrange	0.0	9.0	0.0	0.0	9.0
Rbase	70.0	8.0	70.0	70.0	8.0
Rrange	0.0	12.0	0.0	0.0	12.0
Ac	1.5	3.8	1.5	1.5	3.8
Scale	0.3	0.5	0.3	0.99	0.5
MaxH	90.0	15.0	90.0	90.0	15.0
MaxR	90.0	20.0	90.0	90.0	20.0

6.5.4 Number of Sentinels

For each of the above dynamic fitness landscape behaviors and movement periods, a spectrum of different numbers of population members were assigned as sentinels. The population size for each of the 2-dimensional experiments was 50. Each of the 2-dimensional experimental configurations was run with no sentinels, 5 sentinels, 15 sentinels, 25 sentinels, 35 sentinels, and 45 sentinels, representing 0%, 10%, 30%, 50%, 70%, and 90% of the population respectively. For the 5-dimensional problems, a population size of 200 was used and sentinel experiments were conducted with no sentinels, 20 sentinels, 60 sentinels, 100 sentinels, 140 sentinels, and 180 sentinels, representing the same percentages of the population as for the 2-dimensional problems. For the 10-dimensional problem, a population size of 500 was used and experiments were conducted with no sentinels, 50 sentinels, 150 sentinels, 250 sentinels, 350 sentinels, and 450 sentinels, again representing the same percentages of the population. All experimental configurations were run 100 times and the means and variances of the performance parameters were computed.

6.6 Comparison Experiments

For comparisons of the results, two other types of techniques were examined using each of the dynamic environments and change periods. Triggered hypermutation [27], using a base mutation rate of 0.001 and hypermutation multipliers of 100, 300, and 500, and random immigrants [28], using immigrant factors of 20% and 50% of the population, were examined for each of the dynamic landscape configurations and movement periods.

6.7 Special Static Problems

In Chap. 9 we will examine the usefulness of our new sentinel placement algorithm for population initialization in static EA problems. For these studies we used the 7-dimensional, 5-cone landscape and the 10-dimensional, 14-cone landscape described above. Additionally, we examined the 5-dimensional De Jong test function # 3, the 2-dimensional De Jong test function # 2, and the 10-dimensional Michalewicz function [37]. These last three functions are minimization problems, but were implemented as maximization problems for this study.

6.8 Summary

In this chapter we have described the specific problems to be used in the comparative studies of the sentinel-based EA enhancements described in Chap. 5. There were two different basic static morphologies used. These were implemented with different dimensionality, resulting in five different static morphologies. Each had seven different periods of landscape movement applied, except for the 10-dimensional problem where three different movement periods were applied. Experiments were run for sufficient generations to experience 20 landscape moves. Experiments were conducted on each landscape using 0%, 10%, 30%, 50%, 70%, and 90% of the population assigned as sentinels. Comparison experiments with both triggered hypermutation and random immigrant performance were conducted, using three different triggered hypermutation rates and two different random immigrant percentages, for a total of 341 different basic experimental configurations. Each experiment was run 100 times. Additional experiments were conducted to explore specific interesting results. In the next chapter we will examine the methods we will use for comparing the performance of the different EA enhancements in these experiments.

7

Performance Measurement

7.1 Overview

To properly report results of the experiments described in Chap. 6, we must first resolve some issues related to EA performance measurement in dynamic environments. In this chapter we will address these problems. First we will describe previously used techniques and examine some problems associated with their use. Next we will describe the desired characteristics of performance measurement metrics for dynamic environments. The next section will present our recommended performance evaluation reporting methods and identify how performance will be reported for our experiments. Then we will provide some alternative metrics for standardized reporting of EA performance in dynamic environments, and, finally, we will provide a method for collecting additional dynamic information about EA performance.

7.2 Issues in Performance Measurement

Despite the interest in EAs for dynamic fitness landscapes, there has not been a uniform agreement regarding what constitutes "good" performance for these algorithms. As was discussed in [46] and further elaborated in [44], to analyze and compare the performance of EAs in dynamic fitness landscapes, we must first decide on the appropriate measure of performance.

In the study of EAs in changing environments, extra effort is required in the area of performance measurement. One of the reasons for this is that, when only viewing changes in the population fitness over time, it is not always obvious whether the EA is tracking the fitness landscape optimum or whether the fitness optimum is occasionally revisiting areas of the search space already populated by individuals of the EA. This is especially true when the landscape is multi-modal with many moving peaks. An example of this difficulty can be found in [12], where performance improvements in a dynamic environment are achieved using an EA modification that restricts significant portions of the population to several small regions of the search space when this modification is tested using a test function where the optimum frequently revisits these small regions.

Reviewing our problem analysis discussions, the reason for evaluating EAs in dynamic environments is to enable the construction of EAs that continually provide high-quality solutions to changing problems without the need to retune the EA or have human involvement in the analysis. Good performance, therefore, means that we are interested in the quality of the solutions that an EA provides across the entire range of dynamics that a changing problem might present. With this in mind, let us review what performance measures have been used for EAs in dynamic environments.

Studies of the performance of EAs in dynamic environments have sometimes reported results using traditional measures of EA performance (i.e., off-line performance, on-line performance, and best-so-far curves). These measurements are, in general, not appropriate for measuring EA performance on practical dynamic problems for the following reasons:

- Best-so-far curves are inappropriate, because a population member with a previously discovered "best" value may have a very low fitness after a landscape change.
- Off-line performance measures the running average best-so-far evaluation for each generation. In static landscapes, this measure provides a monotonically increasing value that indicates how rapidly an EA achieves good performance. In dynamic landscapes, however, the use of the "best-so-far" values is inappropriate, because the values are meaningless after a landscape change.
- On-line performance, which measures the average of all fitness function evaluations up to and including the current trial, provides no information about the best values found, which are the values of interest in any practical implementation of an EA in a dynamic environment.

To address these shortcomings, other researchers examining EA performance in dynamic fitness landscapes have suggested the use of the following:

- the difference between the optimum value and the value of the best individual in the environment just before the environment change [64],
- a modified off-line performance measure, where the best-so-far value is reset at each fitness landscape change [12],
- the average Euclidean distance to the optimum at each generation [67],
- best-of-generation averages, at each generation, for many EA runs of the same specific problem, [23], [28], [4], and
- the best of generation minus the worst within a small window of recent generations, compared to the best within the window minus the worst within the window [66].

The first two of these measures require information that severely restricts their use in standardized evaluation of EA performance in dynamic fitness landscapes. They require knowledge of the generation when the fitness landscape changed. In most real problems there may not be any practical way to unequivocally determine that the landscape changed.

The third measure, the average Euclidean distance to the optimum at each generation, is only available in test problems where the exact position of the global optimum in the search space is already known.

The fourth and most common measure, average best of generation at each generation over many runs of the same problem, addresses several of the concerns identified so far. The difficulty in using this measure is that, as mentioned previously, we are interested in the performance of the EA *across the entire range of landscape dynamics*, not just at specific generations. Users of this method usually provide performance curves that can be compared at each specific generation. This method does not, however, provide a convenient method for comparing performance across the full range of landscape dynamics, nor measuring the statistical significance of the results.

The fifth attempt to address performance measurement in dynamic environments is based on an assumption that the best fitness value will not change much over a small number of generations. This measure also does not provide a convenient method for comparing performance across the full range of landscape dynamics.

7.3 Requirements for Performance Measurement

A good performance measurement method for EAs in dynamic environments should have the following characteristics:

- intuitive meaning,
- straightforward methods for statistical significance testing of comparative results, and
- measurement of performance over a sufficiently large exposure to the landscape dynamics so as to reduce the potential of misleading results caused by examination of only small portions of the possible problem dynamics.

7.4 Performance Measurement: Collective Mean Fitness

A new method of dynamic performance is presented here that is related to several previous methods for measuring EA performance in dynamic environments. This method differs from previous methods in the choice of the experimental unit. Since we are concerned with the performance of the EA across the entire range of landscape dynamics, we will consider the experimental unit to be the entire fitness trajectory, collected across EA exposure to a large sample of the landscape dynamics. To begin, we must first define total mean fitness F_T as the average best-of-generation values over multiple runs, further averaged across an infinite number of generations, thereby experiencing all possible problem dynamics. More formally:

$$F_T = \frac{\sum_{g=1}^{G} \left(\sum_{m=1}^{M} (F_{BG}) \Big/ M \right)}{G} = \text{Constant, for } G = \infty. \qquad (7.1)$$

Where:

F_T = the total average fitness of the EA over its exposure to all the possible landscape dynamics
F_{BP} = the best fitness of any peak in the fitness landscape
F_{BG} = the best of generation
M = the number of runs of the EA (100)
G = the number of generations.

It should be noted that as $G \to \infty$, the effect on F_T caused by variation in the best-of-generation fitness value in any specific generation is reduced.

While this might indicate that very large experiments are required for use of this performance metric, the value F_T for an EA approaches a constant after an exposure to a much smaller representative sample of the dynamic environment under the following conditions:

1. The EA has a reasonable recovery time for all types of landscape changes. This means that the EA does not "get lost" for long periods of time and then recover. If the EA did get lost for long periods of time, it would lower the value of the running average of the best of generation, and increased exposure to the dynamics would be necessary to dampen out these reductions.
2. The global maximum fitness can be assumed to be restricted to a small range of values. This means that larger ranges of fitness values require longer exposures to the landscape dynamics to dampen the effect of fitness value fluctuations.

These conditions permit us to define a new measure of performance for use in dynamic fitness landscapes, the collective mean fitness, F_C. This is a single value that is designed to provide an aggregate picture of an EA's performance, where the performance information was collected over a representative sample of the fitness landscape dynamics. Collective mean fitness is defined as the average best-of-generation values, averaged over all of the generations required to expose the EA to a *representative sample* of all possible landscape dynamics, further averaged over multiple runs. More formally:

$$F_C = \frac{\sum_{g=1}^{G} \left(\sum_{m=1}^{M} (F_{BG}) \Big/ M \right)}{G} \approx F_T. \qquad (7.2)$$

The collective mean fitness will approach the total mean fitness after a sufficiently large exposure to the landscape dynamics. The test problems defined in Chap. 6 allow reliable use of this metric after exposure to 20 landscape moves. This is sufficient to allow the stabilization of the running average best-of-generation fitness value to where meaningful performance comparisons can be made. Examples of the dampening of individual fluctuations of the value of F_C over 20 generations using this performance metric are illustrated in Figs. 7.1 and 7.2 for two of the problems used in this study. Figure 7.1 shows the running average best-of-generation value for a population with 30% of the population assigned as sentinels and where the landscape has 14 cones in two dimensions, with all cones are moving chaotically every 20 generations. Figure 7.2 shows the running average best-of-generation value for a population with 90% assigned as sentinels for the 5-dimensional, 5-cone problem, where all cones move in large steps every 10 generations. In these two sample cases it is easy to see the dampening effect of individual best-of-generation values on the F_C value. In all dynamic fitness landscape experiments conducted in this study, EAs are exposed to at least 20 landscape changes, and this amount of exposure to the landscape produces acceptably stable values of F_C. In other problems, where the landscape dynamics may be completely unknown, the number of generations needed to achieve an acceptably stable value for F_C may need to be experimentally established.

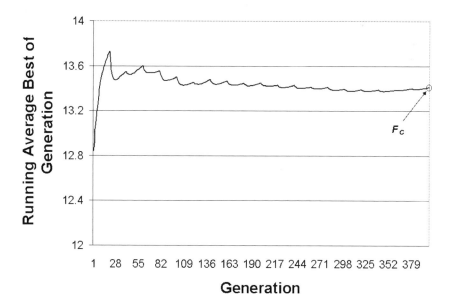

Fig. 7.1. Running average best of generation for 14N2M14C, movement period 20, 30% sentinels

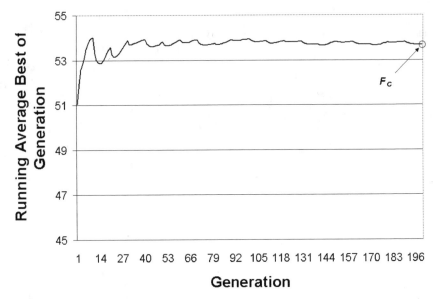

Fig. 7.2. Running average best of generation for 5N5M5L, movement period 10, 90% sentinels

There are two additional items to notice about this performance metric. First, in the case where the fitness landscape changes every generation, this measure is identical to Branke's modified off-line performance [12], if users of the off-line performance metric collect information over a sufficiently large sample of the landscape dynamics. Second, this method of performance measurement is a form of data compression of the performance curves provided in [23], [28], and [4], permitting simple comparison of the performance across the entire dynamic run.

Throughout this study, the collective mean fitness will usually be referred to in an abbreviated form as "collective fitness," and the experimental results will always be averaged over 100 EA runs.

7.5 Alternative Performance Metrics

In some circumstances, it may be desirable to report EA performance relative to a known global best solution. Two variants of the above metric are provided for use in this situation.

Mean fitness error is defined as the difference between the best possible landscape fitness available for each generation and the best discovered fitness in each generation, averaged across the number of EA runs, then averaged over a sufficiently long data gathering period. More formally this is:

$$E_f = \frac{\sum\limits_{g=1}^{G} \left(\sum\limits_{m=1}^{M} (F_{BP} - F_{BG}) \Big/ M \right)}{G}. \tag{7.3}$$

Where:

E_f = the mean fitness error
F_{BP} = the best fitness of any peak in the fitness landscape
F_{BG} = the best of generation
M = the number of runs of the EA (100)
G = the number of generations used to ensure observation of a representative sample of the landscape dynamics.

If the desired measure of performance involves an accurate assessment of the ability of the EA to track a global maximum, mean tracking error is recommended. Mean tracking error is the spatial error between the search-space location of the best of generation and the location of the best fitness peak in the landscape, averaged across the number of EA runs, then averaged over the data gathering period. More formally this is:

$$E_t = \frac{\sum\limits_{g=1}^{G} \left(\sum\limits_{m=1}^{M} \sqrt{\sum\limits_{i=1}^{N} (x_{i,BG} - x_{i,BP})^2} \Big/ M \right)}{G}. \tag{7.4}$$

Where:

E_t = mean tracking error
$x_{i,BG}$ = the x_i coordinate of the best member of the population for the generation
$x_{i,BP}$ = the x_i coordinate of the best peak in the environment for the generation
M = the number of runs of the EA (100)
N = the dimensionality of the search space
G = the number of generations used to ensure observation of a representative sample of the landscape dynamics.

The principal difference between these two measures is that, in multi-modal landscapes, high fitness (and low mean fitness error) can be caused by the EA tracking a peak other than the global optimum. Under these circumstances, an EA can show a low E_f (and a high F_C), while having a high E_t. Use of E_t is, of course, limited to use with test problems where the location of the global maximum is known.

7.6 Additional Summary Dynamic Information

By the same methods used to determine collective mean fitness, other dynamic information can be reasonably collected across an entire experimental trajectory for use in comparing different experiments. One will be useful to us and is defined here as collective dispersion, which is based on the dispersion index, Δ, introduced in Chap. 4. Collective dispersion is the dispersion index at each generation averaged across the number of EA runs, then averaged over a sufficiently long data gathering period for sufficient exposure to the dynamic landscape. Formally:

$$\Delta_C = \frac{\sum\limits_{g=1}^{G} \left(\sum\limits_{m=1}^{M} (\Delta) \Big/ M \right)}{G}. \tag{7.5}$$

7.7 Summary

In this chapter we have addressed appropriate measures of performance for evaluating EAs in dynamic environments and described the measures we will be using to reduce the potential for misinterpreting the effectiveness of any EA enhancements. We have defined a new performance metric for comparing performance information collected across a representative sample of the fitness landscape dynamics called collective mean fitness (or collective fitness) and abbreviated as F_C. This will be the principal performance metric used in our studies, but occasionally other measures will be provided to illustrate some performance information or examine individual parts of experimental runs in more detail.

8

Analysis and Interpretation
of Experimental Results

8.1 Introduction

This chapter will present the results of testing the sentinel-based EA described in Chap. 5, along with other techniques, on the dynamic fitness landscape experiments described in Chap. 6. The results of these experiments provide a basis for establishing the effect of the presence of sentinels on the performance of EAs in dynamic environments. Analysis of these experimental results will assist in identification of the attributes of the sentinel-based EA that alter the performance of the EA, and suggest general methods for improving EA performance in dynamic landscapes.

In this chapter we will first provide an experimental overview of the effect of sentinels on EA performance in dynamic environments. We will next examine performance on the full spectrum of problems previously identified. This is followed by an examination of the performance of the sentinel-based EA relative to both triggered hypermutation and random immigrant techniques, including specific cases where the sentinel-based EA underperforms relative to other known techniques. Next we will further examine the sentinel EA performance, examine the performance improvements resulting from combinations of techniques, and identify the top-performing techniques. Finally, we will use the entire suite of experimental results to illustrate some newly discovered relationships between population dispersion and EA performance in dynamic environments.

8.2 Overview of the Effect of Sentinels

In this section we will provide a brief overview of the effects of using sentinels in a dynamic landscape. As described in Chap. 5, sentinels are full, breeding members of the population. Positioning a part of the population as sentinels in stationary locations throughout the search space allows for "auto-detection" of landscape changes and automatic response to those changes through the selection operator. Whenever a landscape shift occurs, the part of the population that has started to converge near a found peak suddenly finds itself in an area of lower fitness. At this point, sentinels elsewhere in the search space will get an increased opportunity to mate and create offspring that are spread throughout the search space, automatically increasing population dispersion. In this way, sentinels provide an "auto-detection" mechanism for fitness landscape changes, avoiding the pitfalls of other techniques discussed earlier regarding the detection of relevant landscape changes and the false triggering of landscape detection algorithms [46].

It should be noted, however, that in multi-modal fitness landscapes, some sentinels may be situated on sub-optimal peaks and have sufficiently high fitness to be selected for mating even while the remainder of the population is converging on a discovered optimum. In these cases, the offspring of the mating sentinels will increase population dispersion and also slow the convergence rate of the EA.

Figures 8.1 and 8.2 show examples of the effect of having sentinels present in an EA population. Figure 8.1 plots the best of generation for the 14-cone, 10-dimensional problem, with all cones moving chaotically and the landscape shifting every 60 generations (14N10M14C Move 60). Figure 8.2 plots the best of generation for the 5-cone, 2-dimensional problem, with one cone moving slowly and the landscape moving every 20 generations (5N2M1S Move 20). Both of these graphs provide performance for EAs with no sentinels, 10% of the population as sentinels, 30% of the population as sentinels, and 50% of the population as sentinels during the first several landscape moves.

There are two important items to notice in these two figures. The first is that there is a dramatic performance improvement resulting from dedicating even a small percentage of the population as sentinels. The second item is that, among the 10%, 20%, and 30% sentinel performance graphs, the best-of-generation curves cross frequently, and it is very difficult to clearly determine the "best" performance across the run. This further illustrates the need for the collective fitness performance metric defined in Chap. 7. Collective fitness will, therefore, be the principal performance reporting metric for the remainder of our discussion.

The next overview we wish to provide is the effect of the presence of sentinels on population dispersion. Figure 8.3 provides the dispersion index for populations with no sentinels and 10%, 30%, 50%, 70%, and 90% sentinels on the 5-cone, 5-dimensional problem with all five cones moving in large steps every 30 generations (5N5ML Move 30). As would be expected, the lowest dispersion is with no sentinels, whereas with 90% sentinels the population maintains a dispersion near 1.0. Two important items to notice here are related to the effect of using intermediate numbers of sentinels (10% through 70%). The presence of sentinels automatically increases dispersion at each landscape move since, once the optimum has moved away from the converging portion of the population, their selection for mating increases. The second item to notice is that with an increasing percentage of the population dedicated to

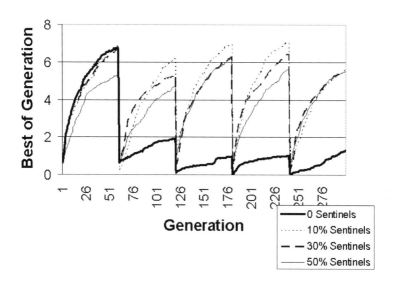

Fig. 8.1. Best of generation, 14N10M14C, move period 60

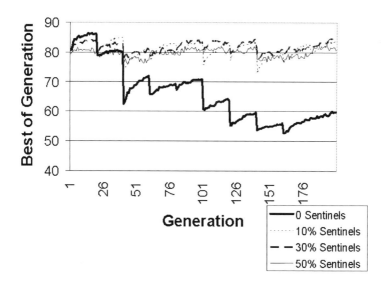

Fig. 8.2. Best of generation, 5N2M1S, move period 20

sentinels, not only does the dispersion increase, but the range of movement of the dispersion index across the run is decreased.

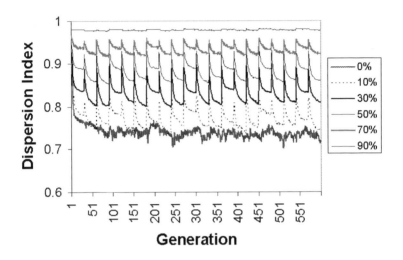

Fig. 8.3. Dispersion index, 5N5M5L, move period 30

8.3 Comprehensive Experimental Results

As discussed in Chap. 6, the problems examined have fundamental differences in their static morphology (including dimensionality), the type of landscape movement, and in the period between fitness landscape changes (as measured in EA generations). In this examination of the effects of sentinels, we will look at the individual test problems under different movement periodicity using differing numbers of sentinels. Figures 8.4 through 8.8 summarize the results of the experiments with the five basic landscape morphologies, across the tested spectrum of different landscape movement periods, without sentinels, and with 10%, 30%, 50%, 70%, and 90% of the population assigned as sentinels. Each of these figures provides, for one landscape morphology, a curve of the collective fitness for each movement period for the different percentages of sentinels. We will examine each of these figures individually and then summarize the common aspects of the results.

Figure 8.4 provides the collective fitness for the easiest of the dynamic problems we examined: the 5-cone, 2-dimensional problem where only the

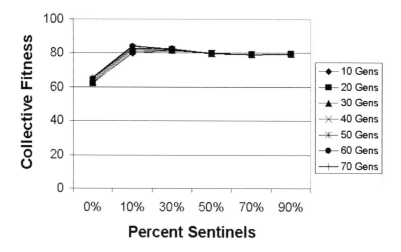

Fig. 8.4. Collective fitness by percent sentinels, 5N2M1S

global maximum is moving, and it is moving in small steps (5N2M1S). As can be seen, the population only requires a small percentage of sentinels (10%) to improve the performance to near the maximum found for each of the movement periods. Except for the very short movement periods where the best collective fitness is found with 30% sentinels, the best collective fitness is found by using 10% of the population as sentinels. With more than 30% sentinels, the performance decreases slightly. Notice that, except for the shortest movement period, the best sentinel percentage for this problem is independent of the landscape movement period (over the range tested). Notice also that in each case the EA is able to find the cone containing the global maximum peak. This is evidenced by the collective fitness being above 70, which is the maximum of the non-optimal cones for this problem, described in Chap. 6. The reduction in performance as the number of sentinels increases appears to be caused by dedicating fewer population members to finding the global maximum on the discovered optimal cone.

Figure 8.5 addresses the other 2-dimensional problem in our test suite, 14N2M14C, in which 14 cones are moving chaotically.

Similar to the results of our first 2-dimensional problem, when only 10% of the population is dedicated as sentinels, a dramatic increase in collective fitness is achieved and the highest cone in the landscape is discovered (evidenced, in this case, by the collective fitness being above 9). In this more complicated problem, however, the period between landscape shifts has more effect on the collective fitness value achieved. For each landscape movement

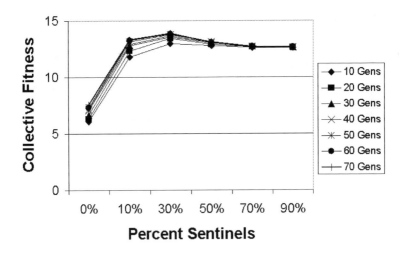

Fig. 8.5. Collective fitness by percent sentinels, 14N2M14C

period, the best collective fitness values are found at 30% sentinels, with a drop-off in collective fitness as more sentinels are used. Again this appears to be caused by a slower search resulting from fewer population members exploring the highest cone.

In Fig. 8.6 we shift our attention to problems of higher dimensionality. Figure 8.6 provides the collective fitness for the 5-cone, 5-dimensional problem, where all the cones are moving in small steps (5N5M5S). Here we see a startling change in that the best collective fitness is found when 70% of the population is dedicated as sentinels. As before, the best percentage of sentinels for one movement period is also the best for all movement periods examined. Collective fitness does not drop off, however, until 90% sentinels are used.

Figure 8.7 shows the collective fitness for a problem similar to that shown in Fig. 8.6, except that all five cones are moving in large steps (5N5M5L).

The problems evaluated in Fig. 8.7 would be expected to be more difficult than those evaluated in Fig. 8.6, but the results appear similar. The principal difference between Figs. 8.6 and 8.7 is that the best choice of sentinels is 50% for the harder problem. Additional information not shown here (but to be discussed later) is that the variances on the collective fitness information are somewhat larger for the more complex problem. As a result, there is a drop in the statistical significance of the results. The differences between the collective fitness values at 50% sentinels and 70% sentinels shown in Fig. 8.6 are statistically significant at the 95% confidence level, except at movement period 70 generations, where the confidence drops to 90%. For Fig. 8.7, the statis-

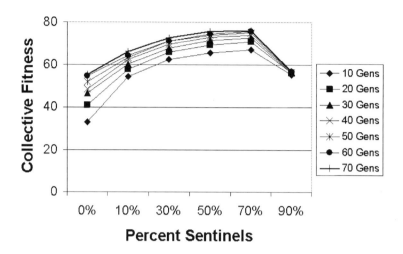

Fig. 8.6. Collective fitness by percent sentinels, 5N5M5S

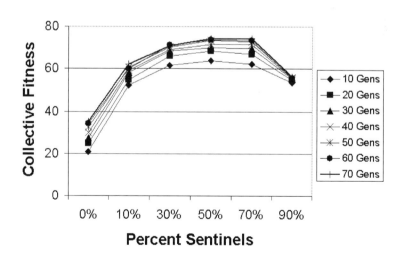

Fig. 8.7. Collective fitness by percent sentinels, 5N5M5L

tical significance of the differences between the fitness values shown for 50% sentinels and 70% sentinels is above the 90% confidence only for movement periods of 10, 20, and 50 generations.

Our final suite of problems is based on the very difficult 14-cone, 10-dimensional problem, where all cones are moving chaotically. Recall that, because of the difficulty of the problem, the population size used for this problem was increased to 500 and the movement periods tested were 30, 60, and 90 generations. The collective fitness results of these experiments are shown in Fig. 8.8.

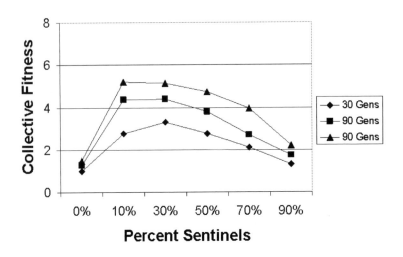

Fig. 8.8. Collective fitness by percent sentinels, 14N10M14C

As seen with previous problems, a small percentage of the population dedicated as sentinels increases the collective fitness considerably. Unlike the previous problems, however, the collective fitness is not above the highest value of the sub-optimal peaks in the landscape, so there is no evidence that the EA is tracking the optimal peak, just that it has found better fitness values. The best collective fitness is found at either 10% or 30% sentinels for these problems. Again, because of the complexity of the problem, the variances of the collective fitness values are higher, so statistical significance of the results becomes an issue. In this case, however, all differences are statistically significant at the 90% confidence level or better, except for the difference between the values for 10% and 30% sentinels for movement periods 60 and 90. This means that 30% appears to be the best percentage of sentinels to use for all movement periods tested, within the statistical significance of the results. These results are consistent with all other problems examined in that there is a single best percentage of the population to assign as sentinels across the range of movement periods tested.

8.3.1 Summary of Collective Fitness Results Using Sentinels

From the results observed so far, the dedication of only 10% of the population makes a large improvement in the performance of a standard EA when the environment is changing. The best percentage of the population to dedicate as sentinels is in the range of 10% to 70%, and appears to depend on the morphology of the landscape and the dimensionality of the problem, and be largely independent of the number of generations between landscape shifts. This is important because, for many real problems, the period between landscape shifts is variable or unknown. It is useful to know that the best percentage of the population to dedicate as sentinels does not vary with this unknown quantity. In the next section we will examine other EA techniques that have been used for addressing moving landscapes on these same problems, and compare the results to those achieved using sentinels.

8.4 Overview of Comparison to Other Techniques

In this section we will examine how two other EA techniques that have been applied in dynamic environments perform on the problems selected for this study. Specifically, triggered hypermutation [15], with hypermutation rates of 100, 300, and 500, and random immigrants [28], with immigrant rates of 20% and 50%, are applied for all morphologies and landscape movement periods. These techniques are abbreviated as Hyp100, Hyp300, Hyp500, Immig20, and Immig50 respectively.

Figures 8.9 through 8.13 provide the results of these alternative techniques on problems 5N2M1S, 14N2M14C, 5N5M5S, 5N5M5L, and 14N10M14C respectively.

These results illustrate that, as with the sentinel enhancements, when a particular technique is best for a morphology, it will generally be the best across the entire range of periods between landscape movements tested. What is less obvious in looking at these figures is that for all problems except the 5-cone, 5-dimensional, large-movement problem, one or more of the triggered hypermutation techniques or random immigrant techniques slightly outperforms all of the different sentinel configurations.

Several additional experiments were conducted to further investigate these performance relationships. The additional experiments will be addressed next and some of the results will be examined in detail.

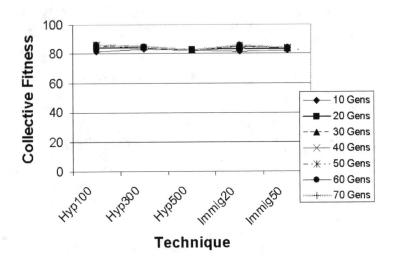

Fig. 8.9. Collective fitness by technique, 5N2M1S

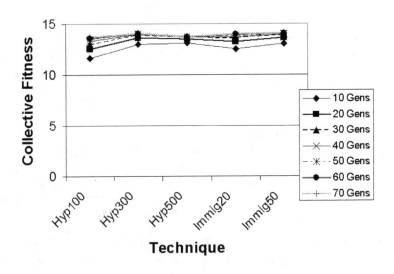

Fig. 8.10. Collective fitness by technique, 14N2M14C

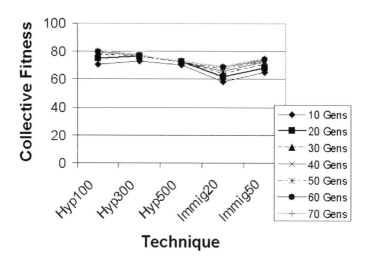

Fig. 8.11. Collective fitness by technique, 5N5M5S

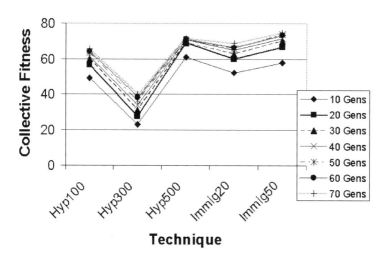

Fig. 8.12. Collective fitness by technique, 5N5M5L

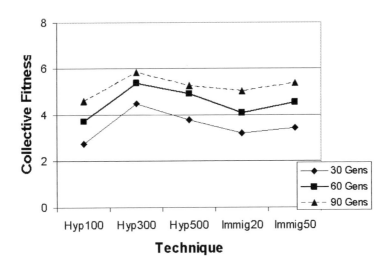

Fig. 8.13. Collective fitness by technique, 14N10M14C

8.5 Comparison Analysis and Combined Techniques

In this section we will perform a more detailed examination of performance differences between sentinels and other techniques on some of the problems tested, and examine the results of combining sentinel techniques with other techniques to achieve performance improvement. We will first examine the 5-cone, 5-dimensional problem where all cones move in small steps (5N5M5S) for all performance periods. For this problem we will add sentinels to the top-performing technique and examine the results. We will then compare these results to the similar 5-dimensional problem (5N5M5L) where sentinel techniques were the top performers.

For the problem 5N5M5S at all movement periods examined, triggered hypermutation, with hypermutation rates of both 100 and 300, outperformed all of the sentinel configurations tested, with a statistical confidence of at least 90%. The difference in collective fitness between these two hypermutation results (rates of 100 and 300) was not statistically significant, due to a fairly large variance for the hypermutation rate 100 results. As a further experiment, 10% sentinels were added to the triggered hypermutation rate 100, essentially combining the techniques (note: just as the sentinels are not modified or replaced by other genetic operators, hypermutation was not applied to the sentinels). Detailed plots of the average best of generation, over 100 runs, for generations 392 to 605 for the experiment with the movement period of 50 generations are shown in Fig. 8.14 for the top four techniques examined.

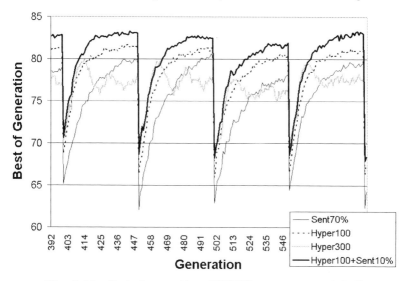

Fig. 8.14. Best of generation, 5N5M5S, movement period 50

In Fig. 8.14, the first item to notice is the performance relationship between the triggered hypermutation 300, the triggered hypermutation 100, and the 70% sentinels. It is clear that after a landscape shift, hypermutation 300 initially climbs the tallest peak at a rate that is faster than hypermutation 100 or 70% sentinels. After this early surge of performance, however, the hypermutation 300 performance deteriorates. This is caused by the fact that the hypermutation triggering is based on identifying a reduction in the moving average of the best fitness, and is subject to false triggering as described in [46]. False triggering of the hypermutation, with a factor of 300, is very disruptive to the continued exploitation of promising areas of the search space. At somewhere between 15 and 30 generations after the landscape shift, the 70% sentinel performance starts to exceed the hypermutation 300 performance. This indicates that, for much longer periods between landscape shifts, the overall performance of the 70% sentinels might be better than hypermutation 300. The use of 70% sentinels on a similar problem could be appropriate if the landscape movement includes very long periods.

As can be seen in Fig. 8.14, the hypermutation rate of 100 is much less disruptive than the hypermutation rate of 300 when false landscape triggers occur. But, as was mentioned earlier, the hypermutation 100 results have a very large variance in the collective fitness and, while appearing to outperform the hypermutation rate of 300, the differences are not statistically significant.

When a combination based on 10% of the population assigned as sentinels and the hypermutation rate of 100 is used, the results change. The variance of the results drops to a much lower level, and the collective fitness of the combined techniques outperforms the hypermutation rate of 300. This is clearly the best choice for this problem.

Figure 8.15 provides some insight into why adding sentinels changed the results. Figure 8.15 shows the average dispersion index over 100 runs, for the same problem as Fig. 8.14. It shows that the combined techniques raised the population dispersion above that for hypermutation 100, without involving as much oscillation in the dispersion index as hypermutation 300 created. All three of these techniques had a much lower dispersion index than 70% sentinels, indicating that the best solutions have neither too much nor too little dispersion.

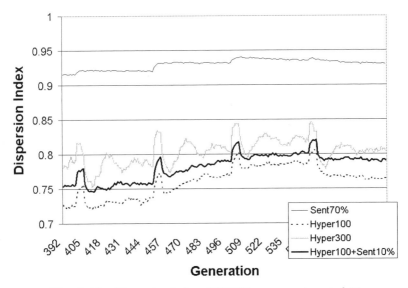

Fig. 8.15. Dispersion index, 5N5M5S, movement period 50

For the 5-cone, 5-dimensional problem where all of the cones are moving large distances (5N5M5L), the use of sentinels matched or exceeded all other techniques examined. To examine these results in detail relative to the similar problem discussed previously, where the cones only moved small distances, Fig. 8.16 shows the same information for 5N5M5L as Fig. 8.14 provided for 5N5M5S.

With this problem, the landscape changes enough with each shift that additional dispersion improves performance. The top-performing techniques for this problem were 50% sentinels, 70% sentinels, 50% random immigrants, and triggered hypermutation with a rate of 500. As with the previous problem, triggered hypermutation starts strongly, but as false triggers of the hypermutation take place, the performance falls off. With a hypermutation factor of 500 (resulting in a 50% mutation rate), the disruption caused by false triggers

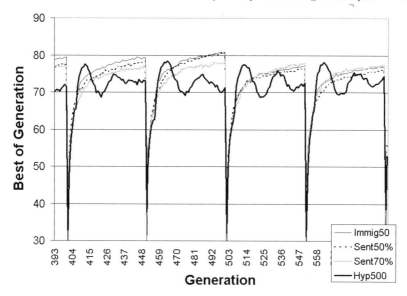

Fig. 8.16. Best of generation, 5N5M5L, movement period 50

is quite severe. Contrast this with the performance of the random immigrants curve. The random immigrants technique uses the same triggering mechanism as triggered hypermutation, and so is subject to the same false activation. In the case of a false trigger, however, randomly replacing 50% of the population is much less disruptive than randomly replacing 50% of the bits in the entire population.

Figure 8.17 shows the average dispersion index for the same movement periods as Fig. 8.16. This figure illustrates the increased dispersion over the previous problem with smaller landscape movements (Fig. 8.15), and illustrates the larger fluctuations in the dispersion index for the triggered hypermutation technique.

With these results we have shown that small changes in the dispersion can be introduced using small numbers of sentinels. Sentinels can be combined with other dispersion-inducing techniques, and small changes in dispersion can improve EA performance for some problems.

8.6 Summary of Top-Performing Techniques

In this section we will provide tables of the top-performing techniques for each problem and movement period combination, along with a summary description of the results of using sentinels. The tables will identify the highest-performing technique as well as any technique that is not significantly different from the highest-performing technique (with a confidence of 90%). The techniques will be abbreviated as follows: SentXX% refers to a population with

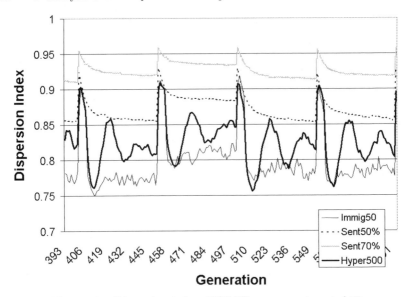

Fig. 8.17. Dispersion index, 5N5M5L, movement period 50

XX% assigned as sentinels, HypYYY refers to triggered hypermutation with a hypermutation factor of YYY, and ImmigZZ refers to random immigrants with ZZ% of the population replaced by immigrants. Combinations of these abbreviations refer to combinations of techniques.

Table 8.1 provides the highest-performing techniques for the 5-cone, 2-dimensional problem where only the global maximum is moving and it is moving in small steps (5N2M1S). As was shown in Figs. 8.4 and 8.9, this is a fairly easy problem and all of the dispersion-introducing techniques performed very well. However, the best-performing technique, by a very small margin, was triggered hypermutation 100 for the longer movement periods and triggered hypermutation 300 for the shortest period. The combination of 10% sentinels with triggered hypermutation 100 achieved a performance level that was not significantly different from the highest-performing technique for movement periods 10 through 50, thereby matching top performance across a broader range of movement periods with a single set of dispersion-introducing techniques.

Table 8.2 provides the top-performing techniques for the 14-cone, 2-dimensional problem where all 14 cones are moving chaotically. Again, with the low dimensionality of this problem, any dispersion-introducing technique finds this problem fairly easy to solve. Although statistically significant differences in performance exist, several other techniques (including combination techniques) performed within 1% of the highest-performing technique. Combining 10% sentinels with a triggered hypermutation rate of 300 only improved

Table 8.1. Best performers, problem 5N2M1S

Problem	Move Period	Technique	Collective Fitness	Variance
5N2M1S	10	Hyp300	83.398337	0.617834
5N2M1S	10	Hyp100Sent10%	82.678230	0.105755
5N2M1S	20	Hyp100Sent10%	84.481460	0.495770
5N2M1S	20	Hyp100	84.354579	0.468284
5N2M1S	20	Hyp300	84.249760	0.414111
5N2M1S	30	Hyp100	85.318792	0.262115
5N2M1S	30	Hyp100Sent10%	85.202460	0.393483
5N2M1S	40	Hyp100	85.967041	0.207045
5N2M1S	40	Hyp100Sent10%	85.432360	0.422461
5N2M1S	50	Hyp100	86.285402	0.095027
5N2M1S	50	Hyp100Sent10%	85.764150	0.238200
5N2M1S	60	Hyp100	86.530710	0.069075
5N2M1S	70	Hyp100	86.686762	0.043518

the statistically significant performance of the triggered hypermutation technique for the shortest movement period.

Table 8.2. Best performers, problem 14N2M14C

Problem	Move Period	Technique	Collective Fitness	Variance
14N2M14C	10	Hyp300Sent10%	13.12665	0.05202
14N2M14C	10	Hyp500	13.08914	0.02681
14N2M14C	20	Hyp300Sent10%	13.63322	0.040282
14N2M14C	20	Immig50	13.62919	0.017673
14N2M14C	20	Hyp300	13.62803	0.030334
14N2M14C	30	Immig50	13.86792	0.015412
14N2M14C	40	Immig50	13.94954	0.018604
14N2M14C	50	Immig50	14.02334	0.018819
14N2M14C	50	Hyp300	14.00289	0.017665
14N2M14C	60	Immig50	14.04828	0.018976
14N2M14C	60	Hyp300	14.04285	0.013077
14N2M14C	70	Immig50	14.08589	0.022156
14N2M14C	70	Hyp300	14.07223	0.010551
14N2M14C	70	Immig20	14.04947	0.023488
14N2M14C	70	Hyp300Sent10%	13.99285	0.016598

As we advance to more complicated problems, Table 8.3 provides the top-performing techniques for the 5-cone, 5-dimensional problem where all five cones are moving in small steps (5N5M5S). In this case, combining techniques resulted in more significant improvements. For movement periods of 30, 50, and 70 generations, when the combined techniques were not employed, triggered hypermutation 100 and triggered hypermutation 300 performance results were not significantly different, due to a high variance associated with the triggered hypermutation 100 results. However, when 10% of the population as sentinels is combined with triggered hypermutation 100, the combined techniques resulted in lower variance and improved performance across most movement periods.

Table 8.3. Best performers, problem 5N5M5S

Problem	Move Period	Technique	Collective Fitness	Variance
5N5M5S	10	Hyp300	73.05765	6.257155
5N5M5S	20	Hyp300	76.20011	1.618374
5N5M5S	20	Hyp100Sent10%	75.66363	2.827813
5N5M5S	30	Hyp100Sent10%	77.79763	12.16223
5N5M5S	30	Hyp100	77.39263	23.25658
5N5M5S	30	Hyp300	76.29691	6.461442
5N5M5S	40	Hyp100	79.01320	13.55045
5N5M5S	40	Hyp100Sent10%	78.99845	13.48464
5N5M5S	50	Hyp100Sent10%	80.00549	3.769604
5N5M5S	50	Hyp100	78.10825	55.03524
5N5M5S	60	Hyp100Sent10%	80.45972	8.301312
5N5M5S	60	Hyp100	79.63556	33.05820
5N5M5S	70	Hyp100Sent10%	80.82889	7.322577
5N5M5S	70	Hyp100	80.60227	14.02157

Table 8.4 provides the results for the top-performing techniques for the 5-cone, 5-dimensional problem where all the cones are moving in large steps. For this problem, assigning 50% of the population as sentinels equals or exceeds all other techniques for all movement periods. Assigning 50% of the population as sentinels provides the only solution that is ranked in the top performers across all tested landscape movement periods. This makes it the best choice for solving a problem of this type, especially under circumstances where the movement period is variable or unknown.

Our last set of experiments involves the 14-cone, 10-dimensional problem where all cones are moving chaotically (14N10M14C). The best-performing techniques are shown in Table 8.5. This problem was of sufficient difficulty that none of the techniques got very far towards finding the global optimum, even with 90 generations between landscape moves. In this case, however, triggered hypermutation 300 was the best-performing individual technique over the landscape movement periods tested. When 10% sentinels were added to triggered hypermutation 300, the combination of techniques appears to perform slightly better, but the difference is not statistically significant at the 90% confidence level.

In summary, these results show that the use of sentinels, or combination of sentinels with other techniques, can improve the performance of EAs on a

Table 8.4. Best performers, problem 5N5M5L

Problem	Move Period	Technique	Collective Fitness	Variance
5N5M5L	10	Sent50%	63.70730	12.35721
5N5M5L	10	Sent70%	62.30344	8.232219
5N5M5L	10	Sent30%	61.54857	12.38115
5N5M5L	20	Hyp500	68.89443	5.51042
5N5M5S	20	Sent50%	68.33925	11.27951
5N5M5L	30	Immig50	70.14993	11.13899
5N5M5L	30	Sent50%	70.01065	13.02968
5N5M5L	30	Sent70%	69.70111	8.262717
5N5M5L	30	Hyp500	69.10901	3.402309
5N5M5L	40	Sent50%	71.61223	15.62015
5N5M5L	40	Sent70%	71.53869	7.212131
5N5M5L	40	Immig50	71.36861	16.46066
5N5M5L	40	Hyp500	70.62410	2.321152
5N5M5L	40	Sent30%	69.21139	18.549569
5N5M5L	50	Immig50	73.89463	14.99154
5N5M5L	50	Sent50%	73.43841	12.61960
5N5M5L	50	Sent70%	72.72958	6.900675
5N5M5L	60	Sent50%	73.84393	12.20954
5N5M5L	60	Sent70%	73.43460	7.239727
5N5M5L	60	Immig50	73.31991	13.75555
5N5M5L	60	Sent30%	71.25630	23.293392
5N5M5L	70	Immig50	74.67485	12.51570
5N5M5L	70	Sent70%	74.52694	5.830526
5N5M5L	70	Sent50%	74.43593	12.54762

Table 8.5. Best performers, problem 14N10M14C

Problem	Move Period	Technique	Collective Fitness	Variance
14N10M14C	30	Hyp300Sent10%	4.541755	1.320294
14N10M14C	30	Hyp300	4.481071	1.297702
14N10M14C	30	Immig50	3.434985	0.960534
14N10M14C	60	Hyp300Sent10%	5.625181	0.904628
14N10M14C	60	Hyp300	5.380463	1.590653
14N10M14C	90	Hyp300Sent10%	6.131994	0.487185
14N10M14C	90	Hyp300	5.818380	0.99327

variety of dynamic fitness landscape problems across a broad range of periods between landscape moves. In the next section we will examine some patterns that appear in the results that lead to some more general conclusions about dispersion levels and fitness performance in these dynamic problems.

8.7 Relationship Between Collective Fitness and Collective Dispersion

At several points in the examination of these experimental results, it appeared that small changes in the collective dispersion resulted in changes in the collective fitness for an individual experiment. To examine this phenomenon, scattergrams of the collective fitness vs. the collective dispersion for all techniques examined were plotted for individual experiment morphologies at individual movement periods. Plots for movement periods 20, 40, and 60 are shown for all problems up through five dimensions, and movement periods 30, 60, and 90 are shown for the 10-dimensional problem. These are provided as Figs. 8.18 through 8.33.

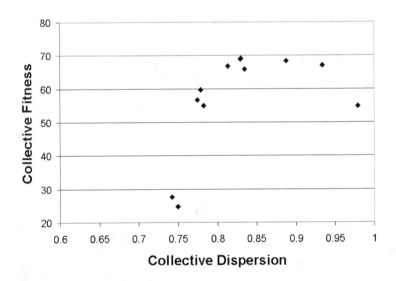

Fig. 8.18. F_C vs. Δ_C, 5N5M5L, move period 20

For the first problem, 5N5M5L, we see a sharp rising edge in collective fitness as collective dispersion increases for all three movement periods (Figs. 8.18 through 8.20). Collective fitness then flattens out for a period of increasing dispersion until eventually collective fitness begins to decline. The collective fitness values vary across the plots with the movement periods, but the shape of the collective fitness curve remains the same.

For both of the 2-dimensional problems, 5N2M1S, where only one cone is moving in small steps, and 14N2M14C, where all cones are moving chaotically, the relationship between collective fitness and collective dispersion is similar to that seen previously, except that there is a larger range of dispersion values

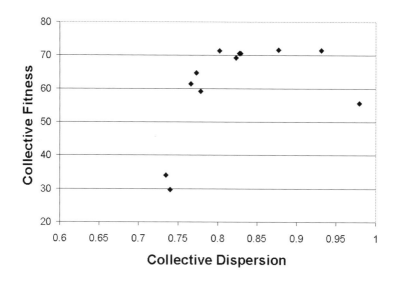

Fig. 8.19. F_C vs. Δ_C, 5N5M5L, move period 40

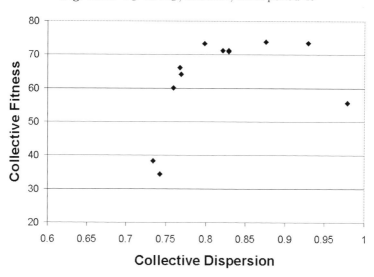

Fig. 8.20. F_C vs. Δ_C, 5N5M5L, move period 60

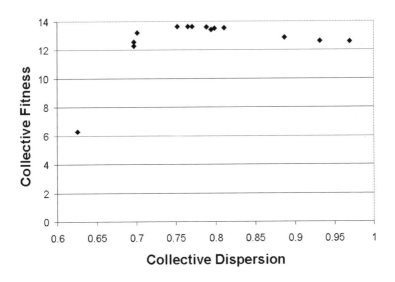

Fig. 8.21. F_C vs. Δ_C, 14N10M14C, move period 20

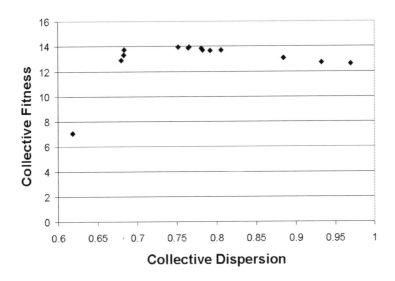

Fig. 8.22. F_C vs. Δ_C, 14N10M14C, move period 40

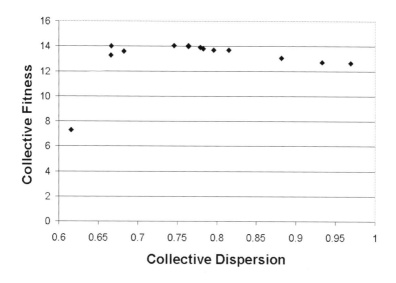

Fig. 8.23. F_C vs. Δ_C, 14N10M14C, move period 60

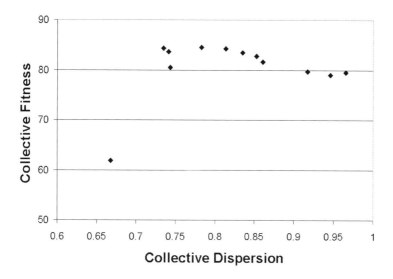

Fig. 8.24. F_C vs. Δ_C, 5N2M1S, move period 20

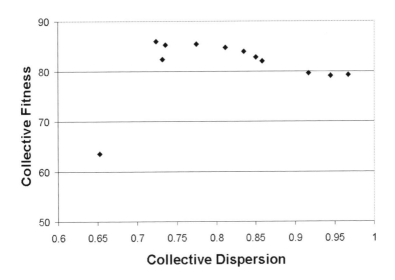

Fig. 8.25. F_C vs. Δ_C, 5N2M1S, move period 40

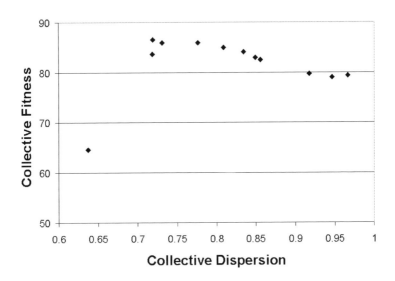

Fig. 8.26. F_C vs. Δ_C, 5N2M1S, move period 60

before a decline in fitness is experienced. The results for these two problems for the various movement periods are provided in Figs. 8.21 through 8.26.

The results for the 5-cone, 5-dimensional problem, where all cones are moving in small steps, are shown as Figs. 8.27 through 8.29. For this problem the relationship between collective fitness and collective dispersion is not quite as clear. The "leading edge" of the plot shows a rise in performance, but has a lot of variability before settling down to the level performance and eventual drop-off seen in the other cases. The difference appears to be caused by some unexpectedly high fitness values for some points. Recalling that this problem's dynamics involve small movements of the cones at each landscape movement, these unexpectedly high fitness values are hypothesized to be related to these small movements. For some landscape shifts, it appears that the global maximum cone moves, but not outside of the boundaries of the converging population, sometimes permitting uninterrupted progress towards discovery of the global maximum.

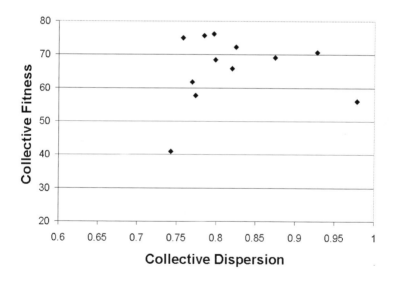

Fig. 8.27. F_C vs. Δ_C, 5N5M5S, move period 20

The final problem examined is the very difficult 14-cone, 10-dimensional problem with all cones moving chaotically. In this case, even though the collective fitness is never high enough to determine that the EA is examining the highest cone in the landscape, the basic pattern of relationship between collective fitness and collective dispersion is the same, with some additional variability at the shortest landscape movement period. These results are shown as Figs. 8.30 through 8.32.

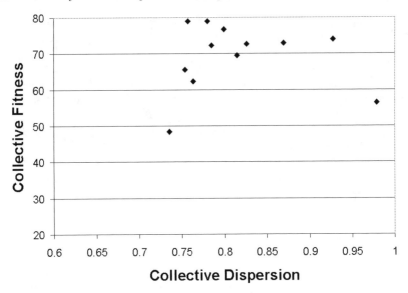

Fig. 8.28. F_C vs. Δ_C, 5N5M5S, move period 40

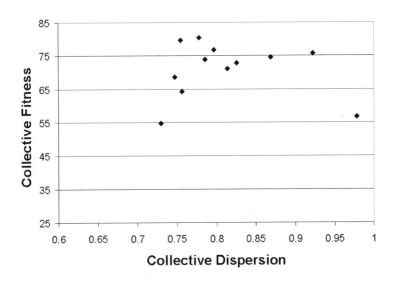

Fig. 8.29. F_C vs. Δ_C, 5N5M5S, move period 60

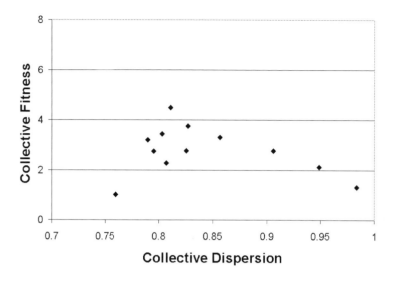

Fig. 8.30. F_C vs. Δ_C, 14N10M14C, move period 30

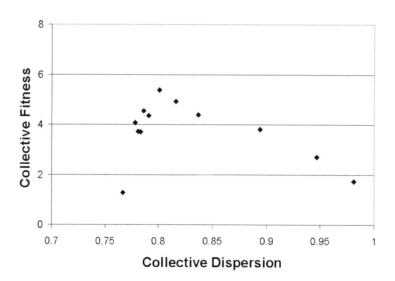

Fig. 8.31. F_C vs. Δ_C, 14N10M14C, move period 60

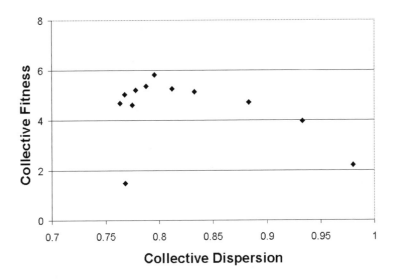

Fig. 8.32. F_C vs. Δ_C, 14N10M14C, move period 90

8.8 Important Dispersion Levels for Different Movement Periods

Throughout the examination of these experimental results, we have observed a relationship between collective fitness and collective dispersion at various movement periods. To further examine this, Fig. 8.33 plots the collective dispersion of the top-performing technique for each problem at the various landscape movement periods.

For all problems except the very difficult, 14-cone, 10-dimensional chaotic movement problem, the best-performing solution showed a general decline through movement periods of 10 through 50 generations (although 5N5M5L showed an unexplained spike in performance at 40 generations). The best-performing solutions then showed a sharp decline in the collective dispersion for periods of 60 and 70 generations. It should be noted that the problems following this pattern had all achieved pretty good results by 50 generations. It therefore appears that the lower level of dispersion required for good performance after this transition point may represent a basic level of population dispersion necessary to solve these problems in the static case, but exploring this possibility will await future research.

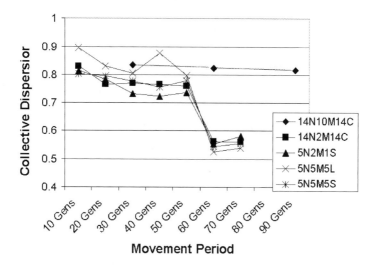

Fig. 8.33. Δ_C values for best problem solutions

8.9 Summary of Experimental Results

The results of these experiments illustrated several items of interest that apply to the problems examined herein. In order of discovery they are:

- Small amounts of dispersion considerably improve EA performance in dynamic landscapes.
- EA performance in dynamic environments is less dependent upon landscape movement period than it is upon available population dispersion. For each landscape morphology, the best population dispersion for one landscape movement period is usually the best across a fairly large range of landscape movement periods.
- Sentinels can provide an effective means of providing the needed population dispersion for good performance in dynamic fitness landscapes, either as a stand-alone technique or as a stabilizing addition to other, more volatile techniques.
- There is a strong relationship between collective dispersion and collective fitness in dynamic landscapes. Progressive increases in collective dispersion will sharply increase collective fitness, then performance will remain steady over a range of collective dispersion values, and then, with further increases in collective dispersion, collective fitness will decline. The exact characteristics of this relationship vary with landscape morphology and movement period, but the general relationship is the same. For some problems, there is some unexplained variation in the data points near the "leading edge"

of the performance improvement curve. This variation is probably related to specific types of small landscape movements re-positioning the global maximum near some of the existing population, but this is unverified at this time. In all cases examined, once past this "leading edge" of the curve, the described performance relationship holds true.

- Finally, the experiments showed a strong relationship between the collective dispersion level of the best-performing technique and the landscape movement period, for most of the problems examined. Except for the very difficult 14-cone, 10-dimensional chaotic movement problem (and one unexplained anomalous point in one of the 5-cone, 5-dimensional problems) the collective dispersion of the best-performing solution showed a general decline through movement periods of 10 through 50 generations and a sharp decline for periods of 60 and 70 generations. This unexplained sharp decline in collective dispersion of the best-performing technique for landscape movement periods longer than 50 generations deserves further investigation.

These experimental results show that collective dispersion levels significantly affect the performance of EAs in a variety of dynamic problems, and have further shown that the collective dispersion levels can be controlled through the use of sentinels. In the next chapter we will revisit the use of the sentinel placement algorithm for population initialization, and in the final chapter we will summarize our research and conclusions.

9

Experimental Results
for Population Initialization

9.1 Overview

In Chap. 5 we suggested that the sentinel placement algorithm that we have developed for our dynamic environment EA might also be useful for population initialization for EAs in static environments. In this chapter, and also in [43], we examine that suggestion by testing a standard EA in a variety of static landscapes using random population initialization and population initialization using the sentinel placement algorithm (referred to as "placed initialization").

9.2 Background

EAs are stochastic search techniques. As such, normal execution of an EA requires many runs to provide reasonable assurance that any negative effects of merely "bad luck" in the stochastic processes have been overcome. One of the first stochastic influences on the behavior of an EA is the population initialization. This has been recognized as a potentially serious problem to the performance of EAs in [32], and, to a lesser extent, in [41] and [12], but little progress has been made in improving the situation. In the few cases where this situation is addressed at all, populations, in very low-dimensionality problems, have been initialized using mathematical techniques like the Latin hypercube [12]. The Latin hypercube technique guarantees uniform placement along each axis, but as was shown in Chap. 5, uniform placement along individual axis projections does not ensure any level of uniformity throughout the search space. In other words, the Latin hypercube technique would provide good values for our intermediate dispersion calculation $\mathbb{S}_1$, but says nothing about the value of the calculation $\mathbb{S}_2$, so it does not ensure uniform search-space coverage, as would be measured by Δ.

Since EAs are generally executed many times to overcome any negative effects of, among other things, the possibility of a bad population initialization, using a better population initialization algorithm would not be expected to improve the average performance of an EA (if executed many times). Instead, it would be expected to reduce the variance without loss of average performance, thereby providing researchers with the opportunity to reliably examine their experimental results while requiring fewer EA runs for an appropriate statistical sample. One would also expect the reduction in variance to be most noticeable in the early generations of the EA run. As was described in Chap. 5, population initialization using the sentinel placement algorithm instead of randomization is not expected to be useful for problems of dimensionality greater than 12 due to the large spatial distances involved. It needs to be reiterated that we are focusing here on average performance. It is conceivable that for some specific problems, more uniform population initialization might actually reduce the peak algorithm performance.

9.3 Experiment

To examine the usefulness of the sentinel placement algorithm for population initialization, a simple EA with gray code binary representation, fitness-proportional selection, uniform crossover, and a mutation rate of 0.001 was used. This EA was run against seven different problems of varying complexity. These problems are:

- De Jong test function #2, also called Rosenbrock's function, in two dimensions [37].
- De Jong test function #3, a step function, in five dimensions [37].
- Michalewicz's function, in ten dimensions [37].
- The 5-cone static landscape used for the dynamic problems described in Chap. 6, in two dimensions.
- The 14-cone static landscape used for the dynamic problems described in Chap. 6, in two dimensions.

A population of 25 was used for the De Jong and Michalewicz test functions and, as in the dynamic landscape problems, a population of 50 was used for the conical landscapes. The De Jong test functions #2 and #3 and the Michalewicz test function are usually implemented as minimization functions, but were implemented as maximization functions for these experiments, applying the following equations respectively:

$$f(\overline{x}) = 3907 - 100(x_1^2 - x_2)^2 + (1 - x_1)^2, \text{ for } x_{1,2} \in [-2.048, 2.048]. \quad (9.1)$$

$$f(\overline{x}) = 25.0 - \sum_{i=1}^{N} |x_i|, \text{ for } x_i \in [-2.048, 2.048]. \quad (9.2)$$

$$f(\overline{x}) = \sum_{i=1}^{N} \left((\sin(x_i)) \left(\sin \left(i x_i^2 / \pi \right) \right)^{20} \right), \text{ for } x_i \in [0, \pi]. \qquad (9.3)$$

The EA was run on each of these problems 100 times using random population initialization and 100 times using placed population initialization (recall that, since the placement algorithm uses a random place for the first placed point, each "placed population" will be different, but equivalently dispersed in the search space). Since these are static problems, the average "best so far," along with its variance, for the 100 runs are reported as the measures of effectiveness in this chapter.

9.4 Experimental Results

The results of the above for the first 25 generations for each of the above experiments are graphed in Figs. 9.1 through 9.10. As can be seen in Figs. 9.1 and 9.2 there appears to be a considerable reduction in variance for De Jong test function #2 and again in Figs. 9.9 and 9.10 for the 14-cone, 2-dimensional landscape. The other charts show less dramatic results, so the results were further analyzed to determine their statistical significance.

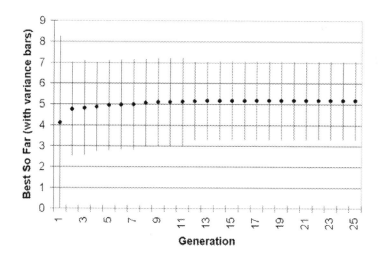

Fig. 9.1. Best so far, random initialization, De Jong test function #2

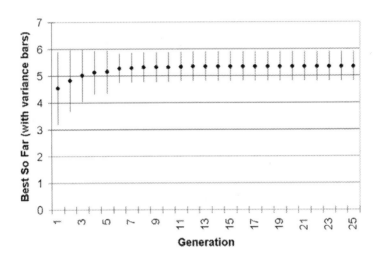

Fig. 9.2. Best so far, placed initialization, De Jong test function #2

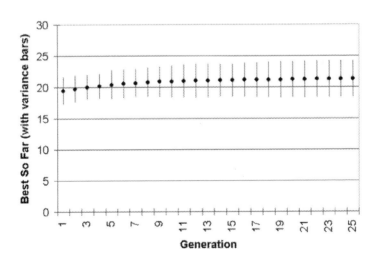

Fig. 9.3. Best so far, random initialization, De Jong test function #3, five dimensions

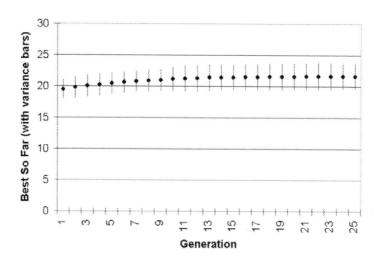

Fig. 9.4. Best so far, placed initialization, De Jong test function #3, five dimensions

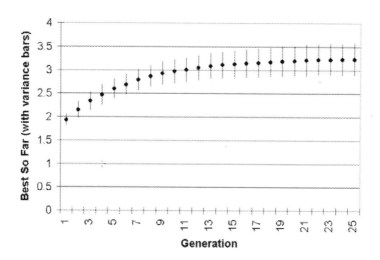

Fig. 9.5. Best so far, random initialization, Michalewicz's function, ten dimensions

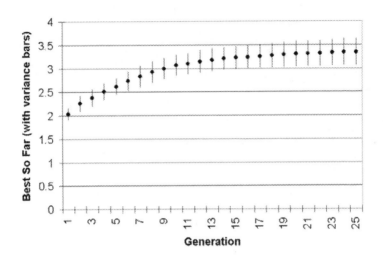

Fig. 9.6. Best so far, placed initialization, Michalewicz's function, ten dimensions

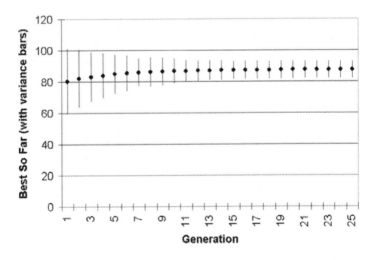

Fig. 9.7. Best so far, random initialization, five cone landscape

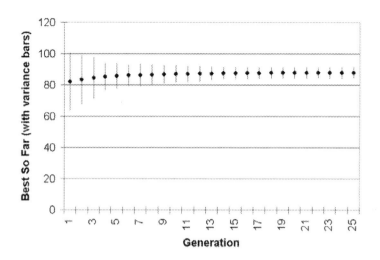

Fig. 9.8. Best so far, placed initialization, five cone landscape

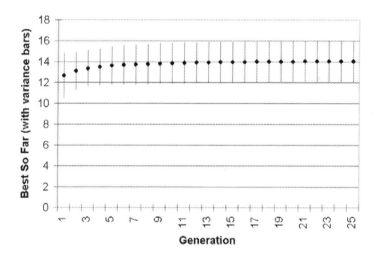

Fig. 9.9. best so far, random initialization, 14 cone landscape

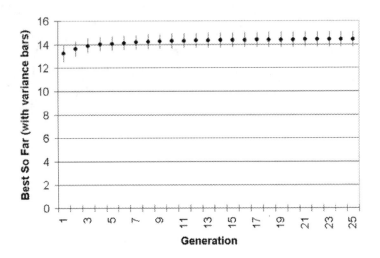

Fig. 9.10. Best so far, placed initialization, 14 cone landscape

9.5 Analysis

At any specific generation, the F-statistic can be used to determine whether the differences between the two variances are statistically significant. This is because the variance at any generation for any single technique is due to the stochastic characteristics of the EA performance and can reasonably be assumed to be normally distributed. In a similar fashion, the t-test can be used to determine if the differences between the average best-so-far values at any specific generation are significant.

Table 9.1 provides a look at the significance of the variance difference seen at generation 10 in each of the figures from the previous section. For each technique, the mean best-so-far (BSF) fitness at generation 10, the variance of the mean fitness at generation 10, the F-statistic computed as the ratio of the squares of the two variances, and the confidence level that the variances are different, are given.

As expected, there was no significant difference in the mean best-so-far performance of the EAs attributable to the population initialization algorithm, but there was generally a reduction in the variance of the mean best-so-far performance. As addressed in Chap. 5, at high dimensions the advantage of the placement algorithm is reduced.

9.6 Summary

In this chapter we have shown the ability of the sentinel placement algorithm developed early as a population initialization mechanism for EAs in static

Table 9.1. Results of different population initialization at generation 10

Test	BSF Mean	Variance	F	Confidence
De Jong 2 2-D random	3905.10	2.12	3.867	99+%
De Jong 2 2-D placed	3905.32	0.55	-	-
-	-	-	-	-
De Jong 3 5-D random	20.90	2.53	1.326	76%
De Jong 3 5-D placed	21.15	1.91	-	-
-	-	-	-	-
Michalewicz 10-D random	3.00	0.26	1.135	77%
Michalewicz 10-D placed	3.10	0.23	-	-
-	-	-	-	-
5-cone 2-D random	86.66	7.79	1.417	89%
5-cone 2-D placed	86.93	5.49	-	-
-	-	-	-	-
14-cone 2-D random	13.83	1.99	3.242	99+%
14-cone 2-D placed	14.29	0.61	-	-

environments. Use of the technique does not improve mean best-so-far performance over a large number of runs. Instead, it reduces the variance of the mean best-so-far performance without loss of average performance, thereby providing researchers with the opportunity to reliably examine their experimental results while needing fewer EA runs for an appropriate statistical sample. This reduction in the required computational resources to achieve reliable experimental results may provide an opportunity for researchers to address more complex problems.

10

Summary and Conclusion

10.1 Summary and Review

The goal of this book was to provide an improved understanding of the design of EAs for dynamic environments as a step towards making EAs capable of satisfactory performance on changing problems without the need for human intervention. As such, this research has served to provide a basis for improving the performance of EAs in dynamic environments, first through derivation of a more meaningful measure of diversity for dynamic environments, called dispersion; second through development and implementation of an extension to EAs, based on concepts from biology and other engineering systems, that allows introduction and maintenance of desired population dispersion levels; and finally through experimental demonstration of the relationship between dispersion levels and EA performance in dynamic environments, over a variety of landscape morphologies and dynamics.

Along the way we also addressed several important design issues regarding the computational efficiency of diversity measurement, the measurement of EA performance in dynamic fitness landscapes, and reduction of the possibility of misleading results caused by lack of a robust test problem generator.

The remainder of this chapter will review the accomplishments of this research, identify some remaining open issues, and suggest specific areas that appear promising for further research.

10.2 Research Results

This section will briefly summarize the results of this research and address the importance of those results to the design of EAs for dynamic fitness landscapes.

- Population diversity is an important factor in the performance of EAs in dynamic fitness landscapes. Traditional population diversity measures are computationally intense. Through an integration of discrete and continuous mathematics, we have devised a computationally efficient method for computing pair-wise Hamming distance, where the computational requirements increase only linearly in population size.

- Traditional population diversity measures used in EA research were developed to measure population convergence in static EA problems, and, therefore, measure the extent to which the population is "not alike." In dynamic fitness landscapes, the important measure of diversity is how well the population is distributed throughout the search space. "Well distributed" is an entirely different concept than "not alike." Exploiting the computational efficiency of our first accomplishment and using the concepts from discrepancy theory, we created a new and computationally efficient measure of how well a population is distributed through the available search space, called the dispersion index, Δ.

- With this new measure of population dispersion, we needed a mechanism to introduce and control this dispersion. Employing some concepts from biology and control systems engineering, we created an extended EA that allows for on-line fine control of population dispersion. Using current research in sequence generation and exploiting the properties of irrational and prime numbers, we designed an algorithm that will place an arbitrary number of points in a space of arbitrary dimension with reasonable uniformity. This algorithm is designed to work throughout the range of population sizes and dimensions normally of interest to the EA community.

- With the invention of a placement algorithm for placing points in a reasonably uniform distribution throughout a search space, we demonstrated that this algorithm is useful for addressing the long-standing problem of population initialization in static EA research.

- Conduct of this research required the creation of dynamic fitness landscapes that provide repeatable experimental environments and easily provide a wide range of dynamic behavior for many types of landscapes in an arbitrary number of dimensions. To accomplish this, we created a dynamic environment problem generator, DF1. This problem generator is designed to expose an EA to dynamic environments of easily controllable levels of complexity where the global optimum is capable of traveling throughout the entire range of the search space.

- To resolve the problems with reported experimental results for EAs in dynamic, multi-modal landscapes, we devised a new performance metric to more accurately measure the performance of an EA over a period of exposure to a range of fitness landscape dynamics.

- We next conducted a comparative experimental evaluation of our extended EA and other techniques in a variety of dynamic environments. We discovered that the level of dispersion to achieve good performance in a specific problem morphology is invariant across a wide range of periods between landscape movements. Identification of this relationship is important for problems where the time between landscape movements is unknown. We discovered that assignment of as little as 10% of the population as sentinels can significantly improve EA performance in some dynamic environments.

- Finally, we identified a relationship between collective fitness and collective dispersion that appears to hold across a range of fitness landscape morphologies and dynamics.

10.3 Open Issues and Suggested Areas for Future Research

While this research has served to address some of the open issues in EA performance in dynamic fitness landscapes, it left many of them untouched and it has also served to open others. The following subsections will describe our recommendations regarding promising areas for further research.

10.3.1 Examination of More Problems

Chapter 8 (Figs. 8.18 through 8.32) indicated a potentially useful relationship between collective dispersion and collective fitness for controlling EA performance in dynamic fitness landscapes. To determine the extent of this relationship, additional problem types will need to be investigated. Of specific concern, very small landscape changes sometimes had an unexpectedly large reduction in collective fitness when using dispersion-enhancing techniques. This area should be further examined, as it could be very important to researchers examining EA operation with noisy fitness evaluations.

10.3.2 Variable Fitness Landscape Change Periods

Results in Chap. 8 (Fig. 8.33) indicate that the best collective dispersion level varies with the fitness landscape change period. Other results in Chap. 8 indicated that, for some problems, sentinels would have outperformed other techniques under longer fitness landscape change periods. Since many real problems have unknown or variable landscape change periods, understanding when to change the dispersion levels requires further study. Understanding of this relationship would permit the automatic adaptation of sentinel deployment strategies in environments with variable change periods.

10.3.3 Additional Capabilities of Sentinels

Since sentinels remain stationary in the fitness landscape across multiple generations, sentinels can be used to provide a more informative picture of the dynamics of the fitness landscape. Specifically, they are able to retain memory of previous fitness values at their search-space location. If they are provided with some limited ability to communicate among themselves, they could derive information about the type and extent of any detected fitness landscape changes. With this information, it may be possible to improve performance by altering the sentinel behavior. For example, if the perceived landscape dynamics indicate a need for more or less dispersion, more or less of the population could be assigned as sentinels. In another example, some of the results in Chap. 8 showed that, in a multi-modal fitness landscape, sentinels sometimes slowed examination of the highest landscape peak by including members from other peaks in the mating pool. It is possible that under some circumstances it might be desirable for sentinels to restrict their mating behavior, based on what they have detected about the landscape dynamics

10.3.4 Additional Combinations of Techniques

Chapter 8 examined several cases of the combination of sentinels with triggered hypermutation to improve results. A further examination of the effectiveness of combined techniques in various environments is warranted.

10.3.5 Selection as a Dispersion Mechanism

Finally, there are other dispersion-introducing mechanisms found in nature that deserve examination for their ability to improve EA performance in dynamic fitness landscapes. One that has not been adequately studied in this context is selection.

Nature provides a variety of complex and subtle mating strategies, many of which do not appear to directly relate to any observable fitness evaluation. In many cases it appears that the males and the females of a population use entirely different criteria for mate selection. One conjecture is that some of these strategies might be related to population dispersion maintenance. A simplified study of this conjecture could be conducted using selection strategies common in EAs.

There are two principal types of selection mechanisms commonly used in EAs: fitness proportional selection and tournament selection. These two selection mechanisms have different behaviors regarding dispersion maintenance, but which is better at maintaining genetic dispersion depends upon the underlying fitness landscape.

A promising area for further research would, therefore, examine the importance of selection as a population dispersion mechanism relative to landscape changes, and examine how the alteration of mating strategies during evolution affects performance in dynamic fitness landscapes.

10.4 Conclusion

The material presented in this book has served to:

1. Resolve open issues in the areas of performance measurement for EAs in dynamic environments.
2. Demonstrate that dispersion is a better search-space coverage metric than diversity, and provide new, computationally efficient methods for both dispersion and diversity measurement.
3. Provide new population placement methods for diversity introduction and maintenance when using either static or dynamic fitness landscapes.
4. Provide a common test problem generator for dynamic environments.
5. Provide experimental indications of the levels of population dispersion important to EA performance in different dynamic environments.
6. Provide an extended EA for dynamic environments which alone, or in combination with other techniques, can significantly improve EA performance.
7. Provide a basis for further research in dynamic environments through better understanding of the role of population dispersion in dynamic fitness landscapes.

Armed with this information, we believe that EA researchers and designers working with EAs in dynamic environments will have a better basis for making design decisions that improve their results.

A

Notation

$\#\{\ldots\}$ the number of times that the expression in $\{\ldots\}$ is true.

A_r the logistic function constant used to change the dynamic behavior of the landscape peak slopes in the test function DF1.

α irrational number.

β a real number.

c_i ith coordinate of a population centroid in N-space.

D Euclidean distance, also D_N when the distance in a specific number of dimensions is required.

$\mathbb{D}_{P(x_P)}$ discrepancy of a sequence of P points.

Δ the search-space dispersion index.

δx a small increment of a real value x.

ε detection range in Euclidean space for an environment change.

E_F fitness error.

E_T tracking error.

F_i fitness of population member i.

F_T the average of the best-of-generation fitness over a representative sample of the dynamic environment.

G the number of generations.

H pair-wise Hamming distance of a binary population.

I an interval on an N-dimensional torus (equivalently an
     N-dimensional interval, modulo 1).

I_C sum of the spatial axes moments of inertia computed from the centroid.

I_{cx} moment of inertia for a single spatial axis x computed from the centroid.

I_0 sum of the spatial axes moments of inertia computed from the origin.

I_{ox} moment of inertia for a single spatial axis x computed from the origin.

J an interval in N-dimensional space.

K the number of participants in K-tournament selection.

k_i the number of ones in column i of a binary population.

L the length of a string.

λ_N N-dimensional Lebesque measure.

M the number of runs of an EA.

N the number of dimensions.

N_P the number of peaks in a landscape using the DF1 dynamic fitness
     landscape generator.

Q the number of alternate population configurations that
     share some identified attribute.

$\Re^N$ N-dimensional real space.

ρ_n the range of the search space along dimension N.

$|S|$ cardinality of the set S or the absolute value of number S.

$\mathbb{S}$ intermediate calculation in the search-space-based dispersion index, Δ.

T^N N-dimensional torus.

x_i the ith spatial coordinate of a point x.

χ_S characteristic function of the subset S of a larger set.

$\mathcal{Z}$ integers.

Z_i an individual integer i.

References

1. Alexander, J. R., Beck, J., and Chen, W. W. L. Geometric discrepancy theory and uniform distribution. In *Handbook of Discrete and Computational Geometry* (1997), J. E. Goodman and J. O'Rourke, Eds., CRC Press, pp. 185–208.
2. American Mathematical Society. What's new in mathematics: the most irrational number. http://www.ams.org/new-in-math/cover/irrational3.html, December 2001.
3. Angeline, P. Tracking extrema in dynamic environments. In *Proceedings of the Sixth International Conference on Evolutionary Programming* (1997), P. J. Angenline, R. G. Reynolds, J. R. McDonnell, and R. Eberhart, Eds., Springer-Verlag, pp. 335–345.
4. Bäck, T. On the behavior of evolutionary algorithms in dynamic fitness landscapes. In *Proceedings of the IEEE International Conference on Evolutionary Computation* (1998), IEEE, pp. 446–451.
5. Bäck, T., and Schwefel, H.-P. An overview of evolutionary algorithms for parameter optimization. *Evolutionary Computation 1*, 1 (Spring 1993), 1–23.
6. Baum, E. B., Boneh, D., and Garrett, C. Where genetic algorithms excel. *Evolutionary Computation 9*, 1 (Spring 2001), 93–124.
7. Beyer, H.-G. *The Theory of Evolutionary Strategies*. Natural Computing Series. Springer-Verlag, 2001.
8. Blackwell, T. M. Particle swarms and population diversity I: analysis. In *2003 Genetic and Evolutionary Computation Conference Workshop Program* (2003), A. Barry, Ed., pp. 103–107.
9. Blackwell, T. M. Swarms in dynamic environments. In *Genetic and Evolutionary Computation - GECCO 2003, Lecture Notes in Computer Science 2723* (2003), E. Cantú-Paz, J. A. Foster, K. Deb, et al., Eds., Springer-Verlag, pp. 1–12.
10. Branke, J. Memory enhanced evolutionary algorithms for changing optimization problems. In *Proceedings of Congress on Evolutionary Computation* (1999), IEEE, pp. 1875–1882.
11. Branke, J. Reducing sampling variance when searching for robust solutions. In *Proceedings of the Genetic and Evolutionary Computation Conference* (2001), Morgan Kaufmann, pp. 235–241.
12. Branke, J. *Evolutionary Optimization in Dynamic Environments*. Kluwer Academic Publishers, 2002.

13. Bratley, P., Fox, B. L., and Neiderreiter, H. Implementation and tests of low-discrepancy sequences. *ACM Transactions on Modeling and Computer Simulation 2*, 3 (July 1992), 195–213.

14. Cobb, H. G. An investigation into the use of hypermutation as an adaptive operator in genetic algorithms having continuous, time-dependent non-stationary environments. Tech. Rep. 6760, Naval Research Laboratory, Washington, DC, 1990.

15. Cobb, H. G., and Grefenstette, J. J. Genetic algorithms for tracking changing environments. In *Proceedings of the Fifth International Conference on Genetic Algorithms* (1993), S. Forrest, Ed., Morgan Kaufmann, pp. 523–530.

16. Darwin, C. *The Origin of Species by Means of Natural Selection.* J. Murray, 1859.

17. Dasgupta, D., and McGregor, D. R. Non-stationary function optimization using the structured genetic algorithm. In *Proceedings of the Second International Conference on Parallel Problem Solving from Nature* (1993), R. Männer and B. Manderick, Eds., Elsevier Science.

18. De Jong, K. *An Analysis of the Behaviour of a Class of Genetic Adaptive Systems.* PhD thesis, University of Michigan, 1975.

19. Drmota, M., and Tichy, R. F. *Sequences, Discrepancies and Applications,* vol. 1651 of *Lecture Notes in Mathematics.* Springer-Verlag, 1997.

20. Eiben, A. E., and Smith, J. E. *Introduction to Evolutionary Computing.* Natural Computing Series. Springer-Verlag, 2003.

21. Elgert, K. D. *Immunology: Understanding of the Immune System.* Wiley-Liss, 1996.

22. Freitas, A. A. *Data Mining and Knowledge Discovery with Evolutionary Algorithms.* Natural Computing Series. Springer-Verlag, 2002.

23. Gaspar, A., and Collard, P. From GAs to artificial immune systems: improving adaptation in time dependent optimization. In *Proceedings of Congress on Evolutionary Computation* (1999), IEEE, pp. 1859–1866.

24. Goldberg, D. E. Construction of high-order deceptive functions from low-order Walsh coefficients. Tech. Rep. 90002, Department of General Engineering, University of Illinois at Urbana–Champaign, 1990.

25. Goldberg, D. E., and Smith, R. E. Nonstationary function optimization using genetic algorithms with dominance and diploidy. In *Proceedings of the Second International Conference on Genetic Algorithms* (1987), Lawrence Erlbaum Associates, pp. 59–68.

26. Goodman, J. E., and O'Rourke, J. *Handbook of Discrete and Computational Geometry.* CRC Press, 1997.

27. Grefenstette, J. J. Genetic algorithms for changing environments. In *The Proceedings of the Second International Conference on Parallel Problem Solving from Nature* (1992), R. Männer and B. Manderick, Eds., North-Holland, pp. 137–144.

28. Grefenstette, J. J. Evolvability in dynamic fitness landscapes: a genetic algorithm approach. In *Proceedings of the Congress on Evolutionary Computation* (1999), IEEE, pp. 2031–2038.

29. Holland, J. H. *Adaptation in Natural and Artificial Systems.* MIT Press, 1992.

30. Holland, J. H. Genetic algorithms. *Scientific American 267*, 1 (July 1992), 44–50.

31. Horn, J. *The Nature of Niching: Genetic Algorithms and the Evolution of Optimal, Cooperative Populations*. PhD thesis, University of Illinois–Champaign, 1997.

32. Kallel, L., and Schoenauer, M. Alternative random initialization in genetic algorithms. In *Proceedings of the Seventh International Conference on Genetic Algorithms* (1997), Morgan Kaufmann, pp. 268–275.

33. Koza, J. R., Bennett III, F. H., Andre, D., and Keane, M. A. *Genetic Programming III: Darwinian Invention and Problem Solving*. Morgan Kaufmann, 1999.

34. Langdon, W. B., and Poli, R. *Foundatioons of Genetic Programming*. Springer-Verlag, 2002.

35. Lewis, J., Hart, E., and Ritchie, G. A comparison of dominance mechanisms and simple mutation in non-stationary problems. In *Proceedings of the Seventh International Conference on Genetic Algorithms* (1997), Morgan Kaufmann, pp. 139–148.

36. Li, Y., Ng, K. C., Murray-Smith, D. J., Gray, G. J., and Sharman, K. C. Genetic algorithm automated approach to the design of sliding mode control system. *International Journal of Control 63*, 4 (1996), 721–739.

37. Liao, Y.-H., and Sun, C.-T. An educational genetic algorithm learning tool. *IEEE Transactions on Education 44*, 2 (2001). CD-ROM Directory 14.

38. Liles, W., and De Jong, K. The usefulness of tag bits in changing environments. In *Proceedings of Congress on Evolutionary Computation* (1999), IEEE, pp. 2054–2060.

39. Marchiori, A., and Steenbeek, A. An evolutionary algorithm for large scale set covering problems with application to airline crew scheduling. In *Real-world Applications of Evolutionary Computation, Lecture Notes in Computer Science 1803* (2000), S. Cagnoni, B. Paechter, T. C. Fogarty, et al., Eds., Springer-Verlag, pp. 367–381.

40. Mardel, S., and Pascoe, S. An overview of genetic algorithms for the solution of optimisation problems. *Computers in Higher Education Economics Review 13* (1999). http://www.economics.ltsn.ac.uk/cheer.htm.

41. Michalewicz, Z., and Fogel, D. B. *How to Solve It: Modern Heuristics*. Springer-Verlag, 2000.

42. Mori, N., Imanishi, S., Kita, H., and Nishikawa, Y. Adaptation to changing environments by means of the memory based thermodynamic genetic algorithm. In *Proceedings of the Seventh International Conference on Genetic Algorithms* (1997), Morgan Kaufmann, pp. 299–306.

43. Morrison, R. W. Dispersion-based population initialization. In *Genetic and Evolutionary Computation - GECCO 2003, Lecture Notes in Computer Science 2723* (2003), E. Cantú-Paz, J. A. Foster, K. Deb, et al., Eds., Springer-Verlag, pp. 1210–1221.

44. Morrison, R. W. Performance measurement in dynamic environments. In *2003 Genetic and Evolutionary Computation Conference Workshop Program* (2003), A. Barry, Ed., pp. 99–102.

45. Morrison, R. W., and De Jong, K. A. A test problem generator for non-stationary environments. In *Proceedings of Congress on Evolutionary Computation* (1999), IEEE, pp. 2047–2053.

46. Morrison, R. W., and De Jong, K. A. Triggered hypermutation revisited. In *Proceedings of Congress on Evolutionary Computation* (2000), IEEE, pp. 1025–1032.

144   References

47. Morrison, R. W., and De Jong, K. A. Measurement of population diversity. In *Artificial Evolution, Lecture Notes in Computer Science 2310* (2002), P. Collet, C. Fonlupt, J.-K. Hao, E. Lutton, and M. Schoenauer, Eds., Springer-Verlag, pp. 31–41.

48. National Oceanographic and Atmospherric Administration. Vostok ice core data for 420,000 years. http://www.ngdc.noaa.gov/paleo/paleo.html, 2002.

49. Neiderreiter, H. Low-discrepancy and low-dispersion sequences. *Journal of Number Theory 30*, 1 (1987), 51–70.

50. Neubauer, A. Prediction of nonlinear and nonstationary time-series using self-adaptive evolution strategies with individual memory. In *Proceedings of the Seventh International Conference on Genetic Algorithms* (1997), Morgan Kaufmann, pp. 727–734.

51. Opera, M. L. *Antibody Repertoires and Pathogen Recognition, the Role of Germline Diversity and Somatic Hypermutation*. PhD thesis, University of New Mexico, 1999.

52. Owen, A. B. Monte Carlo variance of scrambled net quadrature. *Journal of Numerical Analysis 34*, 5 (October 1997), 1884–1910.

53. Press, W. H., Yuekolsky, S. A., Vetterling, W. T., and Flannery, B. P. *Numerical Recipies in C: the art of scientific computing*, second ed. Cambridge University Press, 1997. Reprinted with corrections.

54. Ramsey, C. L., and Grefenstette, J. J. Case-based anytime learning. Tech. Rep. ws-94-07. In *Case-Based Reasoning Papers from the 1994 Workshop* (1994), D. Aha, Ed., AAAI Press.

55. Ronnelwinkel, C., Wilke, C. O., and Martinez, T. Genetic algorithms in time-dependent environments. In *Theoretical Aspects of Evolutionary Computing*, L. Kallel, B. Naudts, and A. Rogers, Eds., Natural Computing Series. Springer-Verlag, 2001.

56. Rush, J. A. Sphere packing and coding theory. In *Handbook of Discrete and Computational Geometry* (1997), J. E. Goodman and J. O'Rourke, Eds., pp. 185–208.

57. Ryan, C. Diploidy without dominance. In *Proceedings of the Third Nordic Workshop on Genetic Algorithms, Helsinki* (1997), Finnish Artificial Intelligence Society, pp. 63–70.

58. Ryan, C., Collins, J. J., and Wallin, D. Non-stationary function optimization using polygenic inheritance. In *Genetic and Evolutionary Computation - GECCO 2003, Lecture Notes in Computer Science 2724* (2003), E. Cantú-Paz, J. A. Foster, K. Deb, et al., Eds., Springer-Verlag, pp. 1320–1331.

59. Shimada, K., and Gossard, D. C. Bubble mesh: automated triangular meshing of non-manifold geometry by sphere packing. In *Proceedings of the Third Symposium on Solid Modeling and Applications* (1995), IEEE, pp. 225–237.

60. Sidaner, A., Bailleux, O., and Chabrier, J.-J. Measuring the spatial dispersion of evolutionary search process: application to Walksat. In *Artificial Evolution, Lecture Notes in Computer Science 2310* (2002), P. Collet, C. Fonlupt, J.-K. Hao, E. Lutton, and M. Schoenauer, Eds., Springer-Verlag, pp. 77–87.

61. Smallwood, R. A two-dimensional Kolmogorov-Smirnov test for binned data. *Physics in Medicine and Biology 41*, 1 (1996), 125–135.

62. Spears, W. M. *Evolutionary Algorithms: The Role of Mutation and Recombination*. Natural Computing Series. Springer-Verlag, 2000.

63. Stephens, C., and Waelbroeck, H. Schemata evolution and building blocks. *Evolutionary Computation 7*, 2 (Summer 1999), 109–124.

64. Trojanowski, K., and Michalewicz, Z. Searching for optima in non-stationary environments. In *Proceedings of Congress on Evolutionary Computation, CEC99* (1999), IEEE, pp. 1843–1850.
65. Varak, F., Jukes, K., and Fogarty, T. Adaptive combustion balancing in multiple burner boiler using a variable range of local search. In *Proceedings of the Seventh International Conference on Genetic Algorithms* (1997), Morgan Kaufmann, pp. 719–726.
66. Weicker, K. Performance measures for dynamic environments. In *Parallel Problem Solving from Nature - PPSN VII, Lecture Notes in Computer Science 2349* (2002), J. J. M. Guervos, P. Adamidis, H.-G. Beyer, J.-L. Fernandez-Villacanas, and H.-P. Schwefel, Eds., Springer-Verlag, pp. 64–73.
67. Weicker, K., and Weicker, N. On evolutionary strategy optimization in dynamic environments. In *Proceedings of the Congress on Evolutionary Computation* (1999), IEEE, pp. 2039–2046.
68. Weisstein, E. World of mathematics. http://mathworld.wolfram.com, 2004.
69. Wilke, C. O. *Evolutionary Dynamics in Time-Dependent Environments.* PhD thesis, Institut für Neuroinformatik, Ruhr-Universität, 1999.
70. Winegerg, M., and Oppacher, F. Distance between populations. In *Genetic and Evolutionary Computation - GECCO 2003, Lecture Notes in Computer Science 2724* (2003), E. Cantú-Paz, J. A. Foster, K. Deb, et al., Eds., Springer-Verlag, pp. 1481–1492.
71. Wolpert, D. H., and Macready, W. G. No free lunch theorems for search. Tech. Rep. SFI-TR-95-02-010, The Santa Fe Institute, 1995.
72. Yi, W., Liu, Q., and He, Y. Dynamic distributed genetic algorithms. In *Proceedings of Congress on Evolutionary Computation* (2000), IEEE, pp. 1132–1135.
73. Yu, H., Wu, A. S., Lin, K.-C., and Shiavone, G. Adaptation of length in a nonstationary environment. In *Genetic and Evolutionary Computation - GECCO 2003, Lecture Notes in Computer Science 2724* (2003), E. Cantú-Paz, J. A. Foster, K. Deb, et al., Eds., Springer-Verlag, pp. 1541–1553.

Index

Natural Computing Series

W.M. Spears: **Evolutionary Algorithms. The Role of Mutation and Recombination.**
XIV, 222 pages, 55 figs., 23 tables. 2000

H.-G. Beyer: **The Theory of Evolution Strategies.**
XIX, 380 pages, 52 figs., 9 tables. 2001

L. Kallel, B. Naudts, A. Rogers (Eds.): **Theoretical Aspects of Evolutionary Computing.**
X, 497 pages. 2001

G. Păun: **Membrane Computing. An Introduction.**
XI, 429 pages, 37 figs., 5 tables. 2002

A.A. Freitas: **Data Mining and Knowledge Discovery with Evolutionary Algorithms.**
XIV, 264 pages, 74 figs., 10 tables. 2002

H.-P. Schwefel, I. Wegener, K. Weinert (Eds.): **Advances in Computational Intelligence. Theory and Practice.**
VIII, 325 pages. 2003

A. Ghosh, S. Tsutsui (Eds.): **Advances in Evolutionary Computing. Theory and Applications.**
XVI, 1006 pages. 2003

L.F. Landweber, E. Winfree (Eds.): **Evolution as Computation.**
DIMACS Workshop, Princeton, January 1999. XV, 332 pages. 2002

M. Hirvensalo: **Quantum Computing.**
2nd ed., XIII, 214 pages. 2004 (first edition published in the series)

A.E. Eiben, J.E. Smith: **Introduction to Evolutionary Computing.**
XV, 299 pages. 2003

A. Ehrenfeucht, T. Harju, I. Petre, D.M. Prescott, G. Rozenberg:
Computation in Living Cells. Gene Assembly in Ciliates.
Approx. 175 pages. 2004

R. Paton, H. Bolouri, M. Holcombe, J. H. Parish, R. Tateson (Eds.):
Computation in Cells and Tissues. Perspectives and Tools of Thought.
Approx. 350 pages. 2004

L. Sekanina: **Evolvable Components. From Theory to Hardware Implementations.**
XVI, 194 pages. 2004

R. W. Morrison: **Designing Evolutionary Algorithms for Dynamic Environments.**
XII, 148 pages, 78 figs. 2004

G. Ciobanu (Ed.): **Modelling in Molecular Biology.**
Approx. 300 pages. 2004

M. Amos: **Theoretical and Experimental DNA Computation.**
Approx. 200 pages. 2004